FAILURE TO THRIVE

FAILURE TO THRIVE

A MEDICAL STUDENT'S NOVEL

C. C. GREEN

NEW DEGREE PRESS
COPYRIGHT © 2022 C. C. GREEN
All rights reserved.

FAILURE TO THRIVE
A Medical Student's Novel

ISBN   979-8-88504-063-1   *Paperback*
            979-8-88504-618-3   *Kindle Ebook*
            979-8-88504-168-3   *Ebook*

For H

"This might have been the only thing that could have awakened you. Your whole life has been a growing from the outside, mastering the challenges that others have set for you. Now, finally, you might just be growing from inside yourself."

—SAMUEL SHEM, *THE HOUSE OF GOD*

"Everybody is a story. When I was a child, people sat around kitchen tables and told their stories. We don't do that so much anymore. Sitting around the table telling stories is not just a way of passing time. It is the way the wisdom gets passed along. The stuff that helps us to live a life worth remembering."

—RACHEL NAOMI REMEN, MD, *KITCHEN TABLE WISDOM: STORIES THAT HEAL*

CONTENTS

AUTHOR'S NOTE 9
CHAPTER 1. ANXIETY 13
CHAPTER 2. SWEATING, EXCESSIVE 25
CHAPTER 3. TARGET OF (PERCEIVED) ADVERSE
DISCRIMINATION AND PERSECUTION 31
CHAPTER 4. FOREIGN BODY 37
CHAPTER 5. INSOMNIA 47
CHAPTER 6. VERTIGO 55
CHAPTER 7. SEMICOMA/STUPOR 63
CHAPTER 8. CHRONIC PAIN 75
CHAPTER 9. ABDOMINAL PAIN 85
CHAPTER 10. FAILURE TO THRIVE 91
CHAPTER 11. WEAKNESS 99
CHAPTER 12. HYPOCHONDRIASIS 105
CHAPTER 13. MENTAL STATUS CHANGES 115
CHAPTER 14. UNSPECIFIED EARLY COMPLICATION OF
TRAUMA 125
CHAPTER 15. IRRITABILITY 135
CHAPTER 16. FATIGUE 141
CHAPTER 17. HEADACHE 151
CHAPTER 18. SYNCOPE 159
CHAPTER 19. HYPERVENTILATION 167
CHAPTER 20. ABNORMAL WEIGHT GAIN 175
CHAPTER 21. HEART FAILURE 183
CHAPTER 22. SHORTNESS OF BREATH 189

CHAPTER 23. SHOCK	195
CHAPTER 24. EPILOGUE	203
ACKNOWLEDGEMENTS	209
APPENDIX	213

AUTHOR'S NOTE

Unloading your emotional baggage on your brand-new roommate isn't a great look, but that's honestly how this book started. As a third-year medical student, I was supposed to be "living the dream." I was *finally* on clinical rotations in the hospital.

In reality, I was "surviving, not thriving." My day had been heartbreaking. I didn't want to talk about it; I normally didn't. I knew all my medical student friends were encountering similar challenges. Sometimes, we would surface-level commiserate, but acknowledging the hard moments was often more exhausting than the initial insults.

Therefore, I quietly dropped my things at the kitchen table while one of my roommates cooked dinner. She was a first-year medical student, taking a break from studying for an exam—one that seemed wildly inconsequential to me after the day I'd had. When she asked how my shift went, I wanted to crawl to my room, write about it in my journal, and forget about it.

Instead, I blurted out: "Can I tell you a story?"

The story isn't important. (You may or may not read it later.) When I finished, we sat in silence for a while.

Eventually, I did go upstairs to lament into a notebook. Later that evening, she sent me a message that made me rethink my usual silence.

"*You know, that story was one of the most inspiring things I have heard since starting medical school. I've sat through who knows how many lectures and small groups, even patient panels, searching for something that reminded me of why we do this. This was the first time in a long time I heard about a real experience.*"

No one talks about being in medical school.

Training to be a doctor must be like *Grey's Anatomy* or *ER*, right? Maybe a chapter from one of Atul Gawande's books? The popular examples all skip right to residency or beyond. Where are the medical students?

The lack of representation is a bit curious. Every year, people are fighting for acceptance to medical school. Over 60,000 people applied for 23,711 seats in 2021 (Boyle, 2021).

Stack that against this statistic: "By the time a student became a resident, sixty percent met the criteria for burnout, and over fifty percent screened positive for depression." (Brazeau, 2014).

Why?

We need to talk about medical school.

Medical students hang in the balance. We study. We take tests. We work long hours. We don't get paid. We're highly educated but clinically useless. Workplace drama and toxic cultures permeate training programs. And that's just in the hospital; imagine having a personal life!

As a medical student, I often questioned whether medicine was what I truly wanted and if I deserved to be there. Losing yourself in the process is easy. I only started to find myself once I started to share my stories. I learned more from my patients. I developed camaraderie with my peers. I began to better understand the needs of the people around me and the potential impact of an empathic physician. I started to enjoy the process of becoming a doctor.

That's why we have to talk about medical school, and that's why we have to share stories.

This book is not only for medical students, to show you that you're not alone. It's for premedical students, to give you a glimpse of the experience. It's for the full-fledged doctors, to remind you of where you've been. It's for the families of those pursuing this career, to give you some insight into our daily lives. Ultimately, this book is for anyone who needs a reminder of what it means to be human.

If no one talks about medical school, then we can't change the shortcomings of the process. More importantly, we can't appreciate the beauty of it, either.

Thank you for the opportunity to share these stories.

C. C. Green

CHAPTER 1

ANXIETY

DANI

Our kitchen table was a piece of shit. Craigslist had, understandably, embellished a bit: "*Contemporary High-Top Dining Table.*" It was much bigger than advertised, surely too big for our tiny home. A warped square of particle board balanced on four legs that wanted so badly to be the same length. Each limb was uniquely nicked and gnawed, and it was hard to tell which joint creaked as the entire structure teetered. The black laminate tabletop was ringed with watermarks, some coalescing like soap bubbles, like a giant-cell tumor of bone on an X-ray.

Yes, I realized that simile was not very accessible. Basically, "soap bubble tumor" is pathognomonic for this one type of cancer…never mind, it doesn't matter. I used to be clever—I was, still, clever—but half of my references and witticisms floated right over the heads of my friends and family. It's as though my brain actively purged all other content to make room for soap bubble tumor factoids. If I made the reference out loud, my roommates would appreciate it. We would all chuckle in mutual self-loathing, at least.

Like internet marketplace ads, our resumés oversold us: "*MD Candidate*." It sounded more legitimate than "medical student" or "student doctor," though, didn't it? Being a medical student felt like a disease sometimes, an ailment that carried a stigma. After seven years in the workforce, I decided to leave my day job as a journalist and my side gig as a bartender to take on crippling debt in pursuit of what? Some higher calling? Because I thought I could "help people" more from a clinic room than from a cubicle? Rotting in the library basement for the first two years of medical school made me less certain.

At thirty years old, I hated to be reminded I was still a student. I did a little hop-skip-jump into my usual seat at the contemporary high-top. A rusted screw dropped from the wood frame and lazily rolled around the cracked tile as I landed firmly on a chair. This shitty table came with only three chairs. Each was falling apart in a slightly different way, just like us.

The coffee maker hissed and sputtered from the countertop. Sam's arms were the only ones long enough to reach the pot without getting up from his seat. Steam fogged the classic black frames over my roommate's bloodshot eyes. He took a sip to ensure the scalding liquid would burn his tongue and winced in confirmation. He would now let it sit until it turned cold, per routine. His curly dark hair was disheveled. I swear he only owned one sweatshirt—a gray crewneck with "MAINE" printed in faded navy across the chest. He'd never been to Maine. The collar was nibbled on one side, and there were small bilateral axillary holes.

Sam had aged a decade since we first met two years ago. He was bright-eyed and bushy-tailed at the beginning of medical school. Now, a couple of gray hairs started peeking out from behind his ears, and the skin around his eyes rested in double parentheticals. He was kind of handsome, in that maybe-someday-he'd-grow-into-his-body sort of way. Despite his skinny arms and legs and self-administered haircut, his teeth sat in perfect rows and completely disarmed anyone if he flashed them. He used this tactic often to mask his awkwardness. It always worked.

His fresh-out-of-undergrad zeal was immediately exhausting. I embraced it for whatever reason, maybe hoping to leech some of his enthusiasm, and we'd been somewhat inseparable since. People in our class thought we were dating for most of the first semester. My girlfriend at the time thought that was hilarious. We were like Sam's second set of parents—his two new moms. Well, until our relationship imploded. Sam thumbed through Reddit on his phone, occasionally smirking and energetically *tap-tap-tapping* his foot despite looking like he otherwise just rose from the dead.

We sat in silence except for Sam clearing his throat every few minutes, a nervous tic that used to irritate me but had become a familiar sound. Our quiet was comfortable. I had trained him to not interrupt me as I worked on the morning crossword, especially the Sunday puzzle. "Okay, g-mom," [translation: grandma] he would say. I would kindly tell him to shut up so I could concentrate. I was the oldest in the house by more than a few years, having recklessly pursued adulthood for a while before committing to medical school, but I was certainly not the "house mom."

The squeak of a rusty handle followed by a series of body slams into the door meant that Anna was home. Right on time. The chalkboard hanging on the wall thudded, and car keys jingled from their hooks. The average burglar would probably give up before gaining entry to our house, but not

Anna. The latch ultimately surrendered, and she fell gracefully into the kitchen, iced coffee in hand, unfazed by this daily obstacle.

"Good morning, sunshines!" Anna cheerily tucked a strand from her dark bob behind her ear. Not shockingly, it always dried perfectly straight without a trace of frizz. *Why is she wearing real pants?* My sweats glared at her slim-fit jeans, neatly cuffed over her shiny loafers. Her taupe-painted fingernails reached for the paper towels. She gently swaddled her perspiring plastic cup before resting it at her place at the table. She had a sparkle in her eyes despite not yet having taken a sip. She would wait until she felt settled, until all three of us were together. Her discipline was astounding.

I brought my five-minutes-empty mug to my lips. "What a glorious day."

Sam still hadn't looked up from blog scrolling. "Living the dream."

"Excellent, excellent," Anna completed our cyclic rhetoric.

I felt a pang of sadness, or maybe anxiety? It was our last day of this routine, the one that carried us through the past two years of "preclinical" med school. I imagined it like a day in Anna's planner, every hour neatly blocked and color-coded. Every day began promptly at 0600 with coffee and complaining, followed by group study, followed by individual study, followed by more group study. We punctuated the monotony with carefully timed meals, always with a side of gossip, and occasionally fit in exercise or other forms of self-care.

Our calendars would look different tomorrow, our first day "on the wards." The next two years of medical school would be spent training on the job. We would be rotating through different hospital departments to gain experience in various specialties before deciding our own fates. We would shuffle through a handful of affiliated hospitals, and each of us would start on a different rotation: Anna on obstetrics and gynecology (Ob-Gyn), Sam on surgery, and internal medicine for me. Our short white coats were pressed, and stethoscopes were tucked into the front pockets.

"Okay, let's go over the schedule for today and what we need for tomorrow..." I half-listened to Anna's play-by-play and checklist, knowing full well that both of us already had our shit together for tomorrow. I humored her. This discussion was more for Sam, who needed handholding.

"Think I need my reflex hammer?" Sam joked.

"Only if you want to look like a dingus." I used one of Sam's favorite words. His eccentric vocabulary somehow became our house vernacular. I wish I had started writing his expressions down earlier in our friendship. Sam's words warranted a dictionary.

"We are all going to look like dingi, it doesn't matter," Sam conceded.

"Din-guy..." Anna tried the plural on for size, "Ha!"

"Well, if you whip out a reflex hammer, you'll look like the king of the dingi." I got up from the table to rinse my mug and grabbed Sam's to pop it in the microwave.

"Can I put that on my CV?"

"Yeah, right under 'worrier-in-chief.'"

"You mean warrior."

"No, I mean—"

"Alright," Anna interjected, "We're leaving in ten to go pick up our scrubs."

"How about twenty?" My phone had just buzzed with a text message from my soon-to-be chief resident, Jay.

"Welcome to the IMC! Please preround on the new patient in the morning and let me know if you have any questions!"

Peppy, I thought, for someone working in the intermediate care unit. The IMC was a step down from the *intensive* care unit, the ICU, but was still quite intensive from what I had heard. Patients had fewer tubes, drains, and devices performing vital organ functions, but some of them were still pretty damn sick. On my first day, thankfully, I was expected to preround on only one patient.

"How about ten?" Anna pushed back.

"Fine, then I need to *pre*-preround on my first patient for tomorrow."

Prerounding—the bane of medical students' existence on most rotations—was a process of information gathering: asking the overnight team about any new developments, reviewing the latest lab results and radiology readings, and collecting any other patient data from the last twenty-four hours.

After receiving Jay's text, I logged into the electronic medical record system from the kitchen table to get a head start, eager to learn about my very first patient of medical school. Nausea set in as I scrolled and scrolled; the patient's medical history was nothing short of a saga. I would need hours to pore over his documents. *What if I'm asked to recite the entire epic for my residents and attending?*

"Dani, it's been ten minutes."

I slammed my laptop closed.

"Let's make this quick…"

SAM

Mission number one. Battle uniform. Hell yes. I led the charge down the hill to the hospital, mostly because the girls had to walk ten paces for each of mine. Having patiently waited my entire life, I was ready to wear scrubs every day. Functional pajamas. The costume of heroes.

We wandered around the hospital for twenty minutes before we found the scrub dispenser. I tapped my shiny new hospital ID to the blinking keypad on the stack of robot doors. The giant vending machine whirred and clicked before unlocking the lowest latch. The one at ground level. For the larges. *Why? Why wouldn't they put the smalls down there?*

I groaned when I bent over, like I had back pain or something, and the girls rolled their eyes on cue. Dani collected her smalls from the top section, which I offered to reach for her so that she didn't have to jump, but she hip-checked me out of the way. The drawstring of Anna's mediums got caught in the hinge on the way out, and the machine screamed at her for holding the door open too long. I imagined a poltergeist inside, cackling as he watched clueless medical students pick up their costumes.

Faded baby blue scrubs now in hand, I peered around the men's locker room cautiously. I chose a nook amongst the rows of lockers where I changed rapidly, as I had for gym class my entire life. Attempting to maintain that level of modesty was perhaps unnecessary, considering I was the only person in there.

When I finished dressing, I stood up as straight as I could in front of the full-length mirror. A startling realization followed: standard-issue hospital scrubs were, ironically, designed to fit absolutely no one. In order to clothe an entire employee population with the full spectrum of body types, scrubs had to be as shapeless as possible.

So, naturally, my upper body was draped in a parachute. *If I were pushed off the roof of the surgical tower, I am ninety-five percent positive that I would land safely.* The V-neck plunged uncomfortably. Without broad shoulders to fill it out, the shirt exposed my sparse dark chest hair and wounded self-esteem. The sleeve circumference was triple that of my biceps. My arms poked out of them like broomsticks.

My lower body, on the contrary, was prepared for a hospital flood. The hems of my pants hung two inches above my ankles when the drawstring was tied around my waist. If I tried to tug them down to hide my white crew socks, then the waistband would slip past my hips. Having no ass meant that the bottoms would slowly make their way down my thighs in an effort to reach my ankles.

How am I supposed to show up on day one and surgerize in these scrubs? Real surgeons often wore their own scrubs, the designer kind that come in "slim fit" and "jogger style." They did not look like dingi in parachutes. I would know. I grew up in a surgeon dynasty.

My moms were both Ivy League-trained general surgeons, as were their fathers. They met at Stanford during their fellowship years. Not being able to procreate worked out well for them, as they didn't have any major gaps in their training and could keep climbing the ladder. They adopted me at the end of their first year as attendings when I was one year old. They joked that all three of us had lived for only a year at that point, that we were all starting our lives. They were good moms, but they were better surgeons.

As a toddler mastering my ABCs, I also learned that "OR" meant "operating room" and "NPO" meant no snacks after dinner. I could tie my shoes using the "bunny rabbit" method, "loop, swoop, and pull," or a classic surgeon's knot. In all my twenty-four years, I had never had a formal doctor's visit. Lacerations were stitched up at the kitchen table, antibiotics dispensed from the household pharmacy, and broken fingers splinted on scene at the playground. When we first learned how to perform a physical exam during medical school, I asked Anna if she had been to the doctor before. She looked at me like I was an alien, then waited for a punchline that I never delivered. *Joke's on me.*

My moms would never admit that I was brought into our family to continue the surgeon dynasty, but years of medical-themed birthday gifts and micromanaged career choices suggested otherwise. Being accepted to only one medical school was the largest disappointment of my upbringing. Over my dead body would they ever find out I was pulled from the waitlist. I wasn't opposed to the idea of becoming a surgeon, but wouldn't I know already if that was my calling? "That's the point of your third year of med school," they assured me, "to figure out what specialty suits you."

Over the next twelve weeks, I was going to be rotating through a handful of surgical specialties to gain exposure to the different fields. This wasn't shadowing anymore. We were trained to interview patients, perform physical exams, and interpret lab tests and diagnostic images. Then we'd synthesize the information to come up with an assessment and plan to present to the residents and attendings (the real doctors). We would scrub into the ORs to assist in surgeries, follow surgical patients who were admitted, and see pre-op and post-op patients in clinic. My sincerest hope and dream for this rotation was that I would fall deeply, madly, irrevocably in love with surgery—to continue the dynasty.

I walked out of the locker room in my scrubs, and the girls burst out laughing.

ANNA

Scrubs, check. Prereading, check. Lunch, check. Next, the class board meeting.

Arriving at the glorified student council session fifteen minutes early, I would have an opportunity to chat with the new fourth-year medical students—the sources for all practical knowledge regarding clinical rotations. Being elected to the board had its perks. As soon as I sat down, one of them asked me what clerkship I'd be starting first. When I revealed "Ob-Gyn," there was a synchronized cringe amongst the elders.

"Raise your hand if you've been personally victimized by Bitchy-Rachel."

The nickname startled me, coming from the mouth of the virtuous class president, one who typically chose careful words over profanity and brushed off unpleasant personalities with optimism. The medical students seated around the conference room shot their hands up like school children eager to tattle.

"She told me that my C-section closure was abysmal."

"She ignored me for six straight days."

"She basically told me to fuck off during a delivery..."

It wasn't just her, the resident generally known as "Bitchy-Rachel." The school administration was supposedly addressing multiple mistreatment issues in the department, and Ob-Gyn was just the latest clerkship to face scrutiny. A couple of years ago it was general surgery, something about instruments being thrown in the OR. Before that it was pediatrics, which boggled me, considering the mild-mannered and cheerful stereotype. Supposedly, a cycle of burnout led to negative attitudes, and it was easy to direct negativity toward the bottom of the totem pole, where medical students resorted to smiling and nodding in most situations.

The school attempted to remedy this by lecturing us about it. The "medical student mistreatment" presentation at clerkship orientation last week looked like a sales pitch at a business meeting. The entire class of new third-year medical students piled into a lecture hall for this talk. Some survey data was chewed up and regurgitated into more digestible morsels. *"More than a third reported mistreatment!"* was projected in fire-engine red across the screen at the front of the room.

Ha, "reported." *How bad does the mistreatment have to be to report it?*

The next slide broke down all the ways we could anticipate potentially being abused: verbal insults, discrimination, sexual harassment, even assault. Public humiliation was the most reported. *Would I report a single comment that made me feel inferior? I don't think so. What would be my threshold? One offense per day? Only if it brings tears to my eyes?*

Sam, seated to my right during the talk, nudged me with his elbow that had already been invading my space. He struggled to contain his limbs within the socially acceptable radius of an auditorium chair. He was smirking and leaned over to whisper to Dani and me: "Think about how fun this will be for us, guys!" Dani chuckled softly at the tone of false excitement in his voice, and I shushed him. I was attempting to listen to the instructions on anonymous reporting, not that I ever would need them. Sam continued under his breath anyway, "We've been bullied our whole lives! Piece of cake. Think about how tough it'll be for the really good-looking people." Dani let out an audible guffaw that drew looks from the row in front of us. I shushed again, both of them this time, with a half-smile. *It can't be that bad, can it?*

CHAPTER 2

SWEATING, EXCESSIVE

SAM

 Drenched. Soaked. Sopping wet. I woke up in a sweat pool the size and shape of the Red Sea. *Am I sick? Is it just hot as hell in this house?* Patting the bed around me, I searched for a dry patch where I could relocate. My eyes stayed closed as I cringed at the moisture beneath me. My shirt was *soggy*. Slipping out of my outer shell while remaining horizontal proved to be a clumsy task. Once free from the damp rag, I scooted over to the other side of the bed and renuzzled my pillow. Then, a deep, aggressive male voice broke the sweet silence of the morning.

 "Wake up, wake up, wake up!"

 This low-pitched bellow was my alarm clock. The booming from my phone effectively scared me awake most mornings.

 "Good thing you never have women over, you lunatic," Dani remarked after hearing it from the kitchen once.

 I thought it was funny—the alarm tone, not the being single part.

 I sat up and stretched my arms to the heavens. *Well, I guess it's time to surgerize.*

A quick shower cured the remnants of my night sweats. *Am I just anxious?* Trying not to look at myself in the mirror too long, I donned my idiotic-looking scrubs and ran my fingers through my wet curls. The kitchen was too quiet as I made my coffee. I would miss the girls this morning, our timing being slightly off for our first-day orientation schedules. It would only get worse; I didn't know if I would see them most mornings.

I asked Anna last night how I would function without her daybreak play-by-play. The guidebook.

"You can text me!" She loved my dependence on her.

"It's not the same."

I drafted the first of many morning texts as I walked to the hospital.

"Day 1, Regret 1: Changing into scrubs at home and walking to the hospital in an unprecedented heatwave."

Lifting my white coat off my chest, I tried to take a photo of the pit stain creeping down my side. As evidence. For the group text.

"Sam!"

The sound of my name startled me, but the nurse passing by wasn't talking to me. I looked over my shoulder and recognized Other Sam. There were two of us in the third-year class. I didn't know him well at all. Our interactions had been limited to a couple of small group workshops. He had been nice enough. Cordial. Pleasant. But we rolled in different crowds. By that, I mean I hung out with Dani and Anna, and Other Sam was cooler than us.

On most rotations during third year, multiple students would be assigned to a particular unit or specialty simultaneously. We would be expected to divide the workload, attend Grand Rounds lectures together, etc. I stopped walking to wait for Other Sam to finish his chat with the nurse. We were going to the same place, after all. He and I would be on the same surgery rotation blocks for the next twelve weeks.

How does he know a nurse already?

Though we were the same height, Other Sam was built like some kind of athlete. Not football...not that thick. And not soccer...not that slim. *What other sports are there?* Regardless, his arms looked thicker than my legs. His dirty blond hair appeared dark in the shade. He must have used some fancy pomade to keep its shape. *Maybe I should have gotten a haircut before today.* Other Sam's hair didn't move at all when he threw his head back to laugh at something the nurse said. As he grinned, I saw the chip in his front tooth, the corner missing as if to intentionally add character. He was clean-shaven, whereas I sported patches of permanent five o'clock shadow. We wore almost identical glasses, but his framed light blue eyes, like robins' eggs.

Ugh, we get it, dude, girls like you. Let's go.

"Hey, man!" He greeted me like an old friend after the nurse walked away, and—for a moment—I felt more popular than I was. "Do you know where we're supposed to go?"

"Hey, dude!" I tried to match his speech. *Too much?* "We're supposed to meet the chief in the resident room. I assume that's the little work area next to the trauma bays, but I'm not sure."

"Cool, cool. Lead the way, boss." He patted me on the back.

Boss? I've never been a boss in my life.

A pair of trauma shears peeked out of the breast pocket of his white coat.

Am I supposed to have those? Shit. All that joking about the reflex hammer, and I'm actually supposed to carry scissors. Small talk, Sam, let's try small talk.

"How was your weekend?"

"It was sweet! Got through the last couple of chapters of DeVirgilio's *Surgery* and played around with the practice question bank for a bit. Just trying to get comfortable with the style of questions, you know? I ripped through some flashcards, too. Otherwise, I just tried to meal prep, hit the gym both days, enjoyed the nice weather..."

I nodded my head in obvious approval as my brain quietly exploded.

He finished the textbook? The textbook for the next twelve weeks?

I understood that we were expected to study as we went through the rotation. The course syllabus recommended a few books but didn't formally require any. We needed to prepare for our cases each day, review any relevant anatomy and physiology, and know some surgical fundamentals for a standardized final exam called the Shelf. *But he's already doing practice questions?* The heat was building in my cheeks as we dropped our bags and sat at the center table in the workroom. I couldn't have been more grateful when the chief resident walked in.

"Are you our new med students?" He was a scruffy character, Dennis Arnold, with bags under his eyes that were likely permanent.

Other Sam stood up, so I stood up.

"Yes, great to meet you. I'm Sam."

"I'm also Sam." I sounded dumb.

"Sam...Also, Sam." Dennis looked us both up and down. It was like he was deciding which of us to adopt from the pound, lost puppies that needed grooming and training. This guy was the "boss" for the next couple of weeks while we rotated through neurosurgery. After that, we'd get a new chief for our four weeks of trauma. It was Dennis' seventh year of residency training. He'd listen to us present patients on rounds and in the clinic, give us feedback, and collect opinions from other team members to ultimately determine our final grades.

"Sweet, same name, but you look nothing alike."

Thanks, Chief. I think we all could agree that it didn't take a literal brain surgeon to notice the difference in our anatomy. I tugged at the hips of my scrubs to try to lower them over my ankles and pulled my white coat closed over my chest.

"I have to go see this one patient quickly; then I'll orient you guys. You can just come with me. She's here for a pre-op appointment. Room four." He cracked open the back door to the clinic and waved us through. Other Sam entered first, then me, then Chief, who whispered from behind me, "Just FYI, she's a bit on edge. I think she has some serious anxiety."

"Don't we all?" I turned and replied under my breath. The chief weakly chuckled, thankfully. When I turned back around, Other Sam was already in the room shaking the patient's hand. And his scrubs seemed to fit just fine.

CHAPTER 3

TARGET OF (PERCEIVED) ADVERSE DISCRIMINATION AND PERSECUTION

ANNA

 Reporting for my first shift at 7:00 meant showing up at the resident room at 6:45, which meant parking around 6:20 to give myself enough time to walk across the entire hospital, change into scrubs, and sit down for morning signout. Leaving the house at 5:45 seemed to minimize room for error. Traffic was inevitable in the city, no matter the time of day. Fifteen minutes, the GPS said, but I didn't trust it. Day shifters would be fighting for parking spots in the garage.

 Maybe 5:30 would be safer.

 Picking up my iced coffee at the neighborhood Starbucks at 5:15, I gave myself more than enough time to get to work. Driving to the affiliated hospital was my first commute experience, and I was ready for it. My medical student podcasts were teed up for the way there, and family phone calls would occupy the ride home. A black plastic hanger now lived in the backseat for my white coat to dangle behind me, avoiding wrinkles.

I can handle this commute, I can handle this rotation, and I certainly can handle Bitchy-Rachel.

The labor and delivery ward was teeming with excitement at 6:42. A flurry of providers hustled through the hallways and every chair was taken in the resident room by someone typing frantically. It was energizing—I was ready to work.

Let's do this.

"Hi, everyone!" I interrupted. "I'm Anna, the new third-year medical student."

Scattered waves and hellos barely interrupted everyone's workflow. The infamous resident glanced over her shoulder and looked me up and down.

"Do you know how to read a strip? You'll be helping the intern."

She didn't even tell me her name. *Does she know her reputation precedes her?* Bitchy-Rachel stood up and walked away with tired purpose, remarking over her shoulder how busy they had been and that I should just try to keep up. She was shorter than I expected, probably a few inches shorter than me. Her dark hair was pulled back into a tight bun that looked painful. Neatly waxed into almost perfectly straight lines, her eyebrows stayed as flat as her tone when she spoke. Though she appeared fit, her scrubs clung tightly around her midsection. *Had anyone mentioned that she is pregnant?*

Yes, of course I knew how to read a strip. By "reading a strip," she meant interpreting an electronic fetal monitor. When a mom comes in to deliver, a sensor is strapped to her belly to measure the response of the baby's heart rate to contractions. I spent a few hours over the weekend reviewing the basics, knowing that I would be tracking labor progress as part of my role.

Admittedly, I actually knew very little about childbirth. During preclinical med school, we learned about fertilization and gastrulation and hormones and fetal development. I knew *those* things quite well, considering we had just taken our first board exam before starting rotations. But I don't think knowing that "the syncytiotrophoblast secretes beta-hCG to maintain the corpus luteum" or that "the notochord induces development of the neural plate from ectoderm" was going to help me deliver a baby.

I had watched a few YouTube videos of live births while sitting at the coffee shop, not even considering that the content would potentially disturb any innocent passersby. I could barely catch a football in the med school's charity powderpuff game. *How am I going to catch a baby?*

Luckily, I was a mere shadow on day one, and shadows don't catch babies. Bitchy-Rachel was right—I was going to have to try to keep up. I closely tailed the intern, a quiet girl who tiptoed around Bitchy-Rachel like a mouse. She saw patients independently, and I was grateful to follow her into and out of rooms to get an idea for the workflow. It was a busy unit, and I was now a member of the team; tomorrow, I would no longer be a shadow, but would be expected to see triage patients, monitor moms in active labor, and gown up to assist with deliveries.

By paying careful attention to every move the intern made—the language she used to talk to moms, the supplies she gathered for each cervix check, the notes she took on her patient list—I readied myself for success. By the fourth patient room, I already pulled her gloves, size 6.5, and laid out her Foley bulb catheter supplies for labor induction before she'd even finished briefing the patient.

"Wow, thanks, Anna!" She smiled with genuine appreciation.

By the end of the day, I felt like I had a good grasp of how the unit operated and how I could be helpful. The intern gave me the green light to head home, knowing full well that she didn't really have the power to do so. I would have to seek out a higher power for true permission. Although it was technically the end of my shift, I still had to be formally released. I had learned from my fourth-year friends how to proceed at this point. I needed to use a certain code, a thinly veiled request for dismissal by a chief resident. I carefully approached Bitchy-Rachel.

"Is there anything else I can help with right now?" *Translation: Can I go home?*

"I don't know, *is* there?" Bitchy-Rachel's eyes were still glued to her computer screen. "I can't believe medical student shifts got shortened. It's fine, we'll all still be here, but go home and do whatever."

Do whatever? Does she mean study, eat, study, sleep, and then arrive promptly back at the hospital? Because that's all that we do, last time I checked.

"Okay! Thanks for everything today. I'll be back at seven."

"Hmm…in the morning?" She still hadn't even looked at me. "It would be better if you did nights this week. The schedule's all fucked up. We'll see you at five p.m. tomorrow for sign-out."

Great. I mean, I will have to rewrite every page of my planner, but that is truly the greatest of my worries.

"Okay! Sounds good. I'll see you at five, then."

I'm glad to do whatever I'm told. If she wants me to come back at 3:47 in the morning, I will be in the parking lot at

2:47 to make sure I have enough time to drink my coffee and mentally prepare myself for any potential suffering.

The junior residents offered a pleasant chorus on my way out the door:

"It was great to meet you today!"

"Thanks for your help!"

"Have a great night!"

But nothing more from Bitchy-Rachel, who was pounding the keys of the desk phone to return a page.

As I stripped off my scrubs in the locker room, I thought about the third of medical students who reported mistreatment. She was a little passive-aggressive, rude, and not the most professional, but was this what people meant by mistreatment? I was certainly going to report my first day to my parents, who were expecting my call. They would definitely want to hear about Bitchy-Rachel. The phone barely rang before they picked up, and their reaction to my story was typical.

"Honey, that's terrible!" My dad, the sweetheart.

"Ha! Oh wow, it's just like when you got bullied by that girl down the street, what was her name, the one who rode the bus?" My mom, the joker, was giggling. She pressed my dad for assistance: "Vin, remember her?"

"Oh, *yes!*"

"Okay—" I interjected. "We are done here. I just wanted to let you know about my first day."

"Honey, we're proud of you. Even if Mean-Rebecca is going to make your life difficult, we know you can get it done."

"It's Bitchy-Rachel, Dad."

"Anna, you were always a tough kid, and you've grown into a strong adult. You've got this."

"Thanks, Mom."

They didn't understand much about medical school. They tried. I really believe they tried. But we didn't have any other doctors in the family. My dad was a grocery store manager; my mom taught second grade. They loved their lives and their kids and their home, but they had no clue what my everyday life had been like since I started this journey. I eventually became too tired to keep trying to explain it.

Everything's fine.

CHAPTER 4

FOREIGN BODY

DANI

Even at zero dark thirty, the hospital looked alive—breathing smoke from rooftop funnels, blinking at the city with scattered eyes, and swallowing workers in rows like ants from the sidewalks. I felt like a foreign body, marching directly into the mouth of a beast.

Rehearsing my presentation in my head, I climbed the stairs to the third floor. *Seventy-year-old male with a past medical history of congestive heart failure, chronic obstructive pulmonary disease, deep vein thrombosis, untreated hepatitis C infection, polysubstance abuse, chronic pain...* With each step I took, I rattled off another condition on his problem list.

During my actual delivery, I would only hit the highlights. No need to get into his history of incarceration and drug rehabilitation, or how he left his last few hospital admissions against medical advice. But, if the attending asked, I would know that he was most recently discharged eight weeks ago, that he had an allergic reaction to Bactrim in 2016, that he preferred chocolate-flavored diet shakes, and that his brother's name was Charles. I knew it was crazy...but we were told to know everything about our patients.

My destination, the resident workroom, was tucked in the middle of the unit across from the nurses' station. Surprised to find it empty, I dropped my things at the least desirable workstation. The dusty one littered with paper clips and old post-it notes, tucked in the corner with the dead lightbulb—that seemed like it would be the designated spot for a medical student. Logging onto the computer, I quickly checked on my patient's chart updates from overnight.

Vital signs...look okay. Labs...also look okay. I think. Thank Christ...there's no more room in my brain for abnormal values. Medication log...hmm...he refused all his medications overnight. Shocker, given his history. I'll have to ask the nurse about that.

I jotted a note on a folded piece of printer paper and shoved it in the front pocket of my white coat.

Alright. Seventy-year-old male...No acute events overnight. Vitals within normal limits. Labs unremarkable. Time to actually meet my first patient.

I knocked modestly, but assuredly, on the very last heavy oak door at the end of the hall.

Click. The release of the door latch was louder than I anticipated. Waiting for an invitation to enter a patient's room was not part of this ritual. We were supposed to barge in and wake them from their slumber. Make them rate their pain from zero to ten and detail their bowel movements. Lay our cold hands on them. *"Knock, knock, sleepyhead! Yes, it's five a.m. No, the real doctor won't see you until around eleven. Welcome to the teaching hospital." Maybe someday this will feel less awkward. Until then...*

"Good morning, sir! My name is Dani. I'll be the student doctor working with your team."

I thought I knew my patient well. Then I met him for the first time.

His voice seemed misplaced, strong-willed and clear, emanating from a small, cachectic figure shrouded by a thin sheet.

"I don't wanna talk. I'm done talkin' ta *you* and done talkin' to the rest of the snakes in this hospital."

Like a snake himself, he writhed onto his back to face me. The room was dimly lit by only the telemetry monitor and the stale glow seeping in from the corridor. When his eyes met mine, I could feel the heat of his electric green gaze, like lasers carving his fury into my retinas.

"Git out."

I parted my lips to attempt a friendly objection. I thought the old foot-in-the-door technique of stammering, "I'm just going to quickly…" before trying to complete my entire history-taking might work. He beat me before I could make a sound.

"I said, *git tha fuck outta my room.*"

I put my hands up in surrender and took slow steps backward as he began thrashing his arms like a mad man.

"*What do you people not understand? You stupid assholes just don't—*"

Click.

After closing the door carefully behind me, I stood there dumbstruck.

Great fucking start.

To be fair, if I were in the hospital, I wouldn't have wanted to talk to a medical student at the ass crack of dawn either. But come on…I spent hours learning about this man. Hours! I'm not Anna or Sam. I needed that time in advance to screw my head on straight, to make sure I understood his medical conditions on my first day. Damn it.

I walked up and down the hallway a couple of times looking for my chief resident, Jay, hoping maybe there was another patient I could see, but no one was around to offer guidance. I returned to the empty resident room.

"Patient uncooperative with interview," I regretfully admitted to the chart.

Drafting progress notes for the day was supposed to close out the process of prerounding. We were expected to form an assessment of patients' clinical statuses and propose a plan for their next steps of care. The plan was often a shot in the dark for medical students, part of the learning experience that the real doctors would ultimately correct during "rounds." *How was I supposed to assess a patient that wouldn't let me touch him?*

"Gooooooood morning!" Jay bounced in. He was exactly as I pictured him, or, rather, exactly how he appeared in his social media photos I'd stalked last night. We exchanged friendly introductions.

"How's your patient?" He asked earnestly with wide eyes.

My heart sank. With so much preparation, I hadn't envisioned being a failure on my very first day.

His expression turned sour as I summarized the encounter.

Jay cautioned me, "If he's agitated, don't attempt an exam…never get too close to his bed. I'm afraid he might swing at you. I just want to make sure there are no safety concerns…" His voice trailed off as he multitasked, logging on to his computer and texting furiously at the same time. "Um… We can go in together to try to rectify this later, or you can just pick up another patient, entirely up to you."

I nodded, unsure of the correct response. He was busy, certainly with more important things than babysitting his medical student.

"You know what," he looked up, "Don't worry about it today. The attending is really nice. Just report what you know about him for rounds."

Rounds included an entire team of medical students, residents, and attendings coming together as a group to discuss every patient assigned to the team. During rounds, I would present each of my patients aloud in a painfully specific format—history of present illness, vital signs, physical exam, labs, imaging, assessment, and plan—to bring everyone up to speed. I would answer any questions posited by other team members; some would be relevant to patient care, some would simply be to test my knowledge. This miserable exercise was known as "pimping." I heard horror stories of medical students being pounded with question after question to expose their ignorance.

This is what I was trying to avoid. I was terrified of being pimped to oblivion. In my career before medical school, I had no fear pitching stories and speaking up in the writer's room. I don't know why this felt so different. Maybe because at some point in this career there would be lives at stake?

If I managed to survive rounds, the team would then divide up work for the rest of the day—talking with consulting services, organizing follow-up appointments, reviewing new labs and imaging, ordering medications, updating family members, writing discharge instructions, etc. That all seemed much less stressful.

Fake it 'til you make it, I told myself when it was my turn.

I confidently presented my failure on rounds. Thankfully, the attending was nothing but understanding and assigned me other patients to see the next day. After rounds, I helped with random tasks for six hours like a glorified secretary. Finally, Jay dismissed me for the day.

Curiosity got the best of me on my way out. My patient's door was propped open. He had apparently lost the privilege of privacy for his behavior. He didn't look away from the television set, tuned to a sports channel, when I knocked.

"Can I get you anything else before I leave for the day?"

"Hmph. How 'bout a fucking fruit cup?"

I felt a flush of anger creep up my neck. *Don't react.* Maybe a peace offering would go further than a lesson on conduct. And a fruit cup seemed reasonable. I had seen fruit cups on other patients' meal trays during rounds. *But where do I get one? Am I allowed to get one?*

I dipped back into the hallway and barely caught my resident. "Jay…"

"Yes…?" He was walking away from me, glancing between his pager in one hand and patient list in the other.

"Can I give my patient a fruit cup?"

"Tell him he only gets a fruit cup if he stops acting like such an asshole."

He turned around, now walking backward, and offered in a more serious tone, "Yeah, I don't see why not." He vanished around the corner. And I still didn't know where to find a fruit cup.

What I thought would be a five-minute good deed turned into a twenty-minute scavenger hunt. When I returned, my patient's head was cocked back so that his snoring reverberated around the room. *So much for a peace offering.* I set his fruit cup on the table next to him. The snack's orange syrup was the only color in the room, like a grayscale photo filter had been applied to the rest. Other patients' windowsills were lined with cards boasting "Get Well Soon!" and "Thinking of You!" Flowers or stuffed animals or balloons filled the bedside spaces. Or family members did.

His bedside drawer was open—in it, a folded pair of jeans and two mini Jolly Ranchers, both green apple, that looked like they had melted and reformed. On the floor next to his bed rested a pair of gray Reebok sneakers. At a closer look, they used to be white. They had matching holes at the toes where the mesh was frayed, and one was missing the insole.

"Just drop him." Jay's words replayed in my head as I walked home. Mr. Fruit Cup had a story, and I couldn't help myself—I loved a good story. I planned on seeing him again in the morning.

* * *

Balancing my travel mug and phone in one hand, clenching the door handle with the other, I rammed my body against the entrance to our home. Anna appeared in the oval window frame, smiling, waving, and allowing me to struggle for another moment before opening the door from the inside. I set my backpack down at my seat in the kitchen.

A small massacre was unfolding on the tabletop. Anna's planner was agape, surrounded by crumpled pages freshly torn from their spiral binding and sticky note tabs ripped from their posts. Her army of colored pens lay in formation, a rainbow platoon positioned at the ready, right next to a fresh iced coffee.

"Isn't it a little late for that?"

In order for Anna to achieve her nine o'clock bedtime, she adamantly avoided caffeine past five.

"Oh, I'm staying up all night. Isn't that fun?"

She could have been an actress if she chose Hollywood over medical school. For someone as serious as Anna—so disciplined and orderly—she had a way of being dramatic.

Bearing an open-mouthed grin that effectively masked the displeasure evident in her tone, she picked up my mug and pranced over to the sink to rinse it.

"Do tell..." I peeped at the fresh ink of her new schedule.

Sam knocked on the window, not even trying to open the door himself. Crouching, he stuck his forehead to the glass, cupping his hand over his head in an attempt to see inside.

"Perfect timing." Anna let him in.

"Hiiiiiiii teammmmm," Sam sang as he dropped his things all over the foyer. "How was day one?"

"Well, I basically got persecuted by Bitchy-Rachel for existing."

"Ooooohhh, how fun!" Sam didn't press for details. "What about you, dingus?"

"Got cussed out of the room by my patient."

"Amazing! Great work, team. Well, everyone showered me with affection, and I'm basically a surgeon already." He pulled books one by one from his backpack and haphazardly stacked them on the kitchen table.

How funny...we had such high and low expectations for our first day. How could we expect so much when we knew so little? And how could we expect so little when we worked so hard for this moment? What bullshit.

Anna handed me a fresh cup of coffee she had already brewed, knowing I would need it to function for the rest of my evening. She returned to our previous discussion. "You're going to stay up all night with me, right?"

"Why are we staying up all night?" I played along.

"Well, if you must know, I was informed at the end of my shift that I'm working nights this week."

Sam and I grimaced in unison.

"Ah, hence the planner wreckage," he noticed.

"It's a good thing you're so flexible!" I joked, playfully jabbing at Anna's rigid routine.

She'll make it work. Sam, on the other hand, worries me. He's already cruising at high speed down the one-way road to burnout, and it's only day one.

"I'm going to shower, then get right to studying," he remarked as he kicked his backpack across the floor toward his room.

"Already?" Anna sounded wounded, hoping that we would hold an extended debrief at the kitchen table.

"This is our life now, sweet girl!" He used her least favorite household nickname to hit home the point. "We'd better get used to it."

"It's a good thing you're so flexible!" I joked, playfully jabbing at Anna's rigid routine.

She'll make it work. Sam, on the other hand, worries me. He's already cruising at high speed down the one-way road to burnout, and it's only day one.

"I'm going to shower, then get right to studying," he remarked as he kicked his backpack across the floor toward his room.

"Already?" Anna sounded wounded, hoping that we would hold an extended debrief at the kitchen table.

"This is our life now, sweet girl!" He used her least favorite household nickname to hit home the point. "We'd better get used to it."

CHAPTER 5

INSOMNIA

ANNA

My third coffee was already pulsing through my veins when Bitchy-Rachel ruined my night with a single text message.

"*Disregard schedule adjustment. Come in for morning sign-out.*"

Is she serious? She can't be serious.

The time stamp read 10:07 p.m.

She's going to text me this late and tell me to be there in less than eight hours?

I had just finished staging my home theater: my laptop screen paused on the introduction slide of an "Abnormal Labor" lecture, a blanket wrapped around my shoulders, and a bowl of popcorn on my lap. If my algorithm was correct—caffeine minus exhaustion divided by anxiety—then I would be up until two or three in the morning. That way, I could sleep all day and set myself up for success in transitioning to night shift.

But apparently I was no longer on night shift, and definitely not set up for success. Bitchy-Rachel clearly had no qualms about destroying my sleep schedule, my spirits, and my planner (for the second time).

"No problem! See you then."

You know what, Anna? You can do this. Tomorrow will be rough. No doubt about it. But get through this lecture, sleep when you can, and reset.

I clicked "play" and attempted to watch the lecture, which I set to double speed. Even with the professor droning on, I knew there was no way I was going to be able to fall asleep. I dialed the first person listed in the favorites section of my contacts. I knew she'd pick up.

My mom answered after one ring.

"Hi, sweetie! How's your late night going?"

"Funny you should ask…I just got a text from my resident to come in for morning sign out."

"So you're not on nights?"

"I'm not on nights."

"So you can go to bed!"

"I wish…I've been caffeinating."

"Oh sweetheart…well, it's only one day and then you can readjust. You will power through!"

Power through. If my parents taught me anything growing up, it was how to power through. How to put my head down and carry on. It's how I survived bullying and heartbreak. How I graduated at the top of my undergrad class. How I made it this far through med school.

"Thanks, Mom."

"Honey, I need to get some sleep, but I'm sure your sister will be up for a while—why don't you call her?"

"Will do. Love you."

"Love you, sweetheart. Remember, power through."

Ugh. I dialed my sister.

"Hey queen!" She answered the same way every time I called.

I'm not sure where she picked that up, but "queen" was a nickname I could tolerate. As kids, we joked that we were secretly princesses—Anastasia instead of Anna and Cinderella instead of Cindy, or her given name, Cynthia, which she despised. Since I'd moved out and my sister still lived at home, my parents revisited our childhood make-believe, joking when it was "Cinderelly's" turn to empty the dishwasher or take out the trash. To me, she was just "C."

"Hi, C."

"Were you just on the phone with Mom?"

"Yes, why?"

"I heard her talking to someone downstairs, and I was trying to listen...she's been sketchy lately."

"What do you mean she's been 'sketchy' lately?"

C had a flair for the dramatic. She often read into things too closely, overanalyzing social situations and coming to her own creative conclusions.

"Well she and Dad have both been sketchy. I don't know how to explain it. Whatever. How's it going with you?"

"Aside from having to switch to days then nights then days, everything's fine!"

She sighed. "You're going to do great, A. You always do. No one is worried about you."

No one ever has been. And why would they be? I've always handled whatever was thrown at me. Never complained out loud. Never showed that I was struggling.

Calling C was a good tactic for staying awake; my sister didn't hesitate to unload on me for a couple hours. Dating drama, friend drama, reality TV drama. I mostly listened with sprinkled reactions—"no way," "oh wow," and "that's wild"—until she abruptly declared that she needed to go to sleep.

My own eyes were finally getting heavy. I closed my laptop, still open to the lecture slides. I had so much to learn.

Like Sam said, "Better get used to it."

Everything's fine.

* * *

At morning sign-out, Bitchy-Rachel confirmed that she and I would *both* be switching to nights next week.

Excellent. Two full weeks of Bitchy-Rachel at every shift. Talk about powering through...

"I'm going to walk around and introduce myself to the laboring moms. You can follow me if you want."

If I "want?" As a medical student, am I allowed to "want" anything? What's the alternative to following you? Sitting here and doing nothing? That's not going to get me honors...

So I followed, into and out of the patient rooms, introducing myself to each of them as the medical student on the team. Some moms got bright-eyed and said some version of "yes, of course, sweetheart!" as if I had asked them permission to be there, which I hadn't. Some treated me as if I were a second grader instead of another adult in their same census age bracket. Bitchy-Rachel looked annoyed during my brief introductions, like I was holding her up.

Isn't this what I am supposed to do? So there's not a stranger in the room while the moms are delivering?

As we reentered the hallway after seeing the last patient, Bitchy-Rachel began walking away from the workroom. I figured maybe there was another patient to see somewhere else, like a consult on another floor, or maybe she needed to talk to a nurse about something. I hadn't been dismissed or directed elsewhere yet, so I did what medical students do best—yes, I followed.

I followed Bitchy-Rachel right to the bathroom.

She whipped around in the doorway just as I noticed the single toilet and sink on the other side.

"Jesus Christ, do you want to come in with me?"

"Oh, I'm so sorry, I wasn't sure where we were going…"

"Well, *I* am going to use the restroom if that's okay with you."

"Of course! I mean, not like you need my permission, I mean, I didn't mean to—"

"You can follow the intern the rest of the day like you did yesterday."

She closed the door in my face.

But you just said to follow you! How was I supposed to know? Did I miss a social cue because I'm too exhausted to function? Ugh.

The rest of the shift, I helped where I could and just tried to stay out of the way. This meant mostly loitering at a computer-on-wheels in the hallway outside the resident room, a crowded storage area for ultrasound machines, utility carts, and medical students. I felt safer from Bitchy-Rachel out there, camouflaged by the other clutter.

"If one more medical student follows me to the bathroom, I'm going to lose my mind." Her voice echoed into the hallway, along with the chuckles of the junior residents.

At least I wasn't the first. And now I know where the bathroom is, not like anyone showed me around.

When it came time for me to gown up for a delivery—the first delivery I would witness in person—I should have been elated. I should have been enthralled. Instead, I could barely keep my eyes open. The blue gown wrapped me in the only warmth I had felt all day, reminiscent of my blanket at home. I tried to focus on everything the intern did, like I did yesterday, but every ounce of focus needed to be directed toward shifting my weight. If I locked my knees and closed my eyes for a second too long, I had no doubt I would hit the floor.

As I plodded to my car at the end of the shift, I called my parents twice, but they didn't answer. *What the heck? They should be home from work already.* I was too tired to really chat anyway; I just wanted to make sure that I stayed awake on my ride. Though I knew exactly how to get home from the hospital, I plugged the address into my phone so I could watch my ETA and anticipate the traffic.

Ding!

Sam texted as I pulled out of the parking garage. *He can wait. Focus on the road.*

Ding!

Ding!

Ding!

If it had been anyone else—anyone—texting me so incessantly, I would have been concerned about an emergency and pulled over to respond. But it was just Sam. I waited until I safely parked at home about a half hour later to read the texts.

"Hi."

"Hiding in bathroom."

"Question."

"Actually many questions."

"1. Have you started practice questions for Shelf?"

"2. When am I supposed to give this midcourse feedback form to someone?"

"3. Are you home yet?"

"4. Can we talk through our schedules when I get home?"

"5. *Why the royal eff did we sign up for this?*"

As I expected, it was not an emergency. I replied in a single organized text:

"1. *No.*
2. *Midcourse.*
3. *Yes.*
4. *Yes.*
5. *Not sure.*"

In regard to his first question: Shelf was the name of the subject exam at the end of each rotation, licensed by the same organization that created our board exams. At the conclusion of the block, Sam would take the exam on surgery, Dani on internal medicine, and I on Ob-Gyn, so it wasn't like we could help each other prepare. We could study in the same vicinity for moral support, but our schedules were so variable that our typical shared misery might not even happen very often.

What is Sam so worried about? Shelf is weeks away. We'll create our shared spreadsheet. I'll plot out our targeted number of practice questions per day, just as we did during preclinical studying. He should know by now that I—that we—would have a plan.

After getting settled, I started to empty the dishwasher, as was my job. I tried making a joke out of it *one time.* "*Why am I always the one to empty this?*" Then it became my job. Dani would help if she happened to be in the kitchen when I started doing it. She preferred a tidy home, having lived by herself for however many years before med school, which I appreciated. Sam, on the other hand, was still learning to do his own laundry. He even had a mug that lived in the dishwasher.

The permanent residence of the Café du Monde mug was on the top rack, back left corner. It had been there for two years, since we first moved in. A thick coffee stain blackened the otherwise chalky white cup. At first, the three of us kept sticking it back in the dishwasher in hopes that it would come clean after another cycle. That went on for months. When I eventually assumed my role as official dishwasher emptier, which I took very seriously, I went to hand wash the mug. "Don't you dare!" Dani stopped me. "Let him wash his own mug." She knew it would drive me mad and that it wouldn't bother him at all; he would just use a different mug. I had to pretend that it didn't bother me. So, the mug lived in the dishwasher. At least I could close the machine and forget it was there, until next time.

CHAPTER 6

VERTIGO

DANI

In a single week, Mr. Fruit Cup earned his reputation as "the impossible one." He flung a meal tray across the room with impressive force when he learned of his new low-salt diet. He got right in Jay's face during rounds and dubbed him "the arrogant fuckin' ringmaster of this goddamn circus of fuckin' clowns." I thought that was pretty clever. He refused medications, physical therapy, social work consultations, chaplain services, and any basic human interaction. It was no wonder he hadn't been showing much clinical progress.

Every morning, I greeted him airily as I wrote "Student Doctor: Dani" on the whiteboard across from his bed—as if he could forget the first person to aggravate him each day. We had a routine now. It went something like this:

"Good morning, sir!"

"*Hmph.* What's so fuckin' good about it? *Huh?*"

Or sometimes:

"Good morning, sir!"

"If one more person wakes me up outta my sleep, Imma start cracking necks out here."

Or maybe:
"Good morning, sir!"
"Christ Almighty, you fuckin' pest. *Git out!*"

I would attempt to assess him, he would berate me, I would try to negotiate, and he would kick me out. Maybe I was "the impossible one."

As stubborn as I was, I didn't have time for a verbal beating before rounds. Not in the middle of my morning from hell. Our team had picked up enough new patients overnight to fill the unit, and Jay was away at a research conference. Somehow, this meant that the intern and I would cover the entire floor.

On top of that misfortune, I would be the first to give a lecture to ten other medical students during our weekly education session. Just when I thought the classroom learning bullshit was over, we got our weekly didactic schedules. Throughout the clinical rotation, medical students would take turns pretending to be subject matter experts on topics we had never diagnosed or treated ourselves. A "teaching resident" would pretend to listen before grading our presentations on a paper rubric. I was up past midnight creating handouts, which meant I was too tired to lay out a business casual outfit for my presentation before bed. That meant that I needed to iron my shirt in the morning, which meant I skipped breakfast and forgot my lunch.

I will be accepting no verbal beatings on a day like today. No, thank you.

Without knocking, I marched through Mr. Fruit Cup's open door and made a declaration. "Good morning. I need to do a quick physical exam on you, and then I'll be going. I'll be back to check on you again later."

"Hmph. An exam of what?" He grumbled.

"Well, a few things…like listen to your heart…"

"Damn it," he interrupted, "well, just get on with it already."

I stepped right up to his bedside. Positioning the earpieces of my stethoscope, I waited for an objection. I remembered Jay's warning not to get too close.

Will I be able to move away fast enough if he tries to hit me?

I held my breath. As I placed the drum of my stethoscope on his chest, I felt my pulse in my fingertips. My heartbeat was certainly faster than his. He didn't move. He didn't say a word. He just glared at me.

Well, if he knocks me out, I won't have to give my presentation this morning.

"Thank you," I murmured after a few beats and pulled away.

"Hmph."

I quickly wrapped up Mr. Fruit Cup's physical exam, then saw my other patients, each more pleasant and cooperative than the last. Hurriedly, I collected my things to run over to the conference room for my talk. I planned to use my five-minute commute to compose myself. As soon as I stepped into the hallway, I realized that wasn't going to happen.

I fumbled with the screaming pager in one hand and failed to balance my lukewarm coffee and meticulously curated handouts in the other. I opted to save every drop of my breakfast and sacrificed my stack of papers. They slid across the floor and scattered themselves throughout the hallway. One sliced an appreciable paper cut into my most useful fingertip on the way down. I hastily bent over to scoop them up.

Pop!

I froze. *Is that what an ACL tear sounds like? Does anything hurt?* Still hunched over, wide eyed, and terrified that I had somehow hurt myself, I conducted a quick survey. After patting my knees, hips, and lower back as I stood up cautiously, I realized what exactly had occurred. My underwear ripped in half inside my pants.

Shit, shit, shit.

I finished collecting my handouts from the filthy floor. The clock above the nurses' station bitched that I was already two minutes late for my presentation. I had no choice but to power-walk across the hospital with two triangular cloth flaps dangling from a waistband inside my plaid slacks.

How? How did this happen?

While speeding down a stairwell, through a bustling lobby, and between stretchers occluding the ICU corridor, I managed to gulp down my caffeine and text Anna, "SOS."

She replied promptly. *"Chief complaint?"*

"Involuntarily commando at work. Visibly bunching fabric at suprapubic area and upper ass crack."

She didn't answer within five seconds, so I clarified. *"I bent over, and my thong ripped in half inside my pants."*

"Hahahahahaha."

Not helpful.

"Good luck on your presentation," she offered facetiously.

I turned into the conference room. Medical students sat around the massive oak table waiting for my lecture on vertigo. *This is not a big deal. Fifteen minutes and you're done.* I reminded myself that this talk was relatively inconsequential. The stakes were much lower when presenting to peers than on rounds. None of us really knew anything, leaving little room for criticism and correction.

"What are some causes of vertigo?"

I attempted to engage my audience members, most of whom were taking the opportunity to shove food into their mouths or nap with their eyes open. A beautiful chart titled "*Causes of Vertigo*" sat at the top of my handout. A copy rested in front of every person in the room. Some even stared blankly at it. When I received no response, I answered it myself:

"Some causes of vertigo include benign paroxysmal positional vertigo, vestibular neuritis, being a medical student lost on the wards…"

Faint smiles crept across a few faces. *Ugh, hated that. Tough crowd.* As I turned to scribble the list of causes on the whiteboard, I remembered my underwear casualty and decided to get through the rest of my talk as quickly as possible.

I concluded by asking if anyone had questions, knowing full well that no one would raise a hand. The teaching resident expressed that she loved my handout as she folded it neatly, then dropped it in the recycling bin on her way out. I saved the extras just to make my backpack heavier; I would never look at them again.

I trekked back to the unit. The faster I walked, the more aware I became of my bulging underwear remains and the tightness of my pants. Stopping at the supply closet would be imperative.

I scoured the shelves for some sort of undergarment. *There had to be something.* My eyes swept over the liters of saline, IV supplies, and boxes of facial tissue. The door creaked open behind me, and a cold draft, unsympathetic to my circumstances, drifted in. Kate, the benevolent nurse, followed it.

I began rifling through the bandages, pretending that I sought something less embarrassing.

"Hey, Dani." She pulled up beside me and began plucking materials off the shelves without even looking—pure muscle memory. "How's your morning?"

"Oh, just breezy." I continued to fumble with random supplies.

She looked at the surgical tape in my hands and furrowed her brow.

"Can I help you find something?"

Screw it. I don't have time for this.

"Um...are there spare underwear of some sort?"

I didn't offer further clarification. She reached above my head, standing on her tiptoes. Her arms were tanned and toned. Her fingers, long and slender, gingerly grasped a bright yellow box on the top shelf. She must have sprayed some kind of perfume on her wrists—subtle and natural. When her elbow brushed me on her way down, my stomach flipped. My palms dampened, and the hair on the nape of my neck stood on end. *Did I just get butterflies?* It had been a while. I couldn't remember the last time a rush of neurotransmitters gave me a belly full of monarchs. I remembered that it was very much not the time as she handed me high-waisted mesh postpartum briefs.

"Breezy, huh?" She smirked.

In the bathroom, I slipped off my flats and slacks, putting my pants around my neck like a scarf because there were two holes in the back of the door instead of a hook. I ditched the thong scraps, wrapping them in a forest's worth of paper towels and shoving them to the bottom of the trash can. I begrudgingly donned the massive briefs. *One size fits all, my ass.* I had to roll and tuck four inches of extra material into my waistband.

Back to fucking work.

As I emerged from the restroom, the secretary saw me and shook her head. At first, I thought my supply closet acquisition had been found out. *Maybe Kate said something?* Then

I heard the yelling. Aggressive shouts echoed from the room at the end of the hall. Mr. Fruit Cup.

He was refusing his medications again. I started walking in the other direction, away from his room. I needed to review my new patients before rounds. I needed to refresh my memory on advanced liver disease. The intern had recommended watching a video on how to perform a paracentesis just in case I was offered the opportunity to do it myself later that afternoon—not that I would get my hopes up. I had too much to accomplish and simply not enough time. I pulled my to-do list from my breast pocket. My own notes scribbled on the page looked foreign.

"*Dani!*"

Mr. Fruit Cup's nurse, having reached a new level of exasperation, appealed to me from his doorway. "I am *done* with him. Can you do something?"

Can I do something? I am the baby, the infant of the unit, appropriately swaddled in a diaper. I'm not getting paid to be here, like the rest of them. I am actually paying for this torture, almost a whopping seventy grand a year. The attending is going to be here any minute for rounds. What am I supposed to do?

Suddenly it felt like it was ninety degrees in the hallway. I ripped off my white coat and tossed it onto the chair outside Mr. Fruit Cup's room.

As I entered, he yelled: "You can't make me do *nuthin'*!" He spitefully turned on his side to face away from me.

Of course, I can't! I can barely gather enough dignity to keep coming into this room every day. What am I even trying to prove?

I inhaled slowly and deeply as I willfully walked around to the other side of his bed. I crouched down in front of him to level our eyes and procured my calmest voice. "You know what? You are right. I can't make you do anything."

His eyes flickered with their usual fire and fury.

I refused to look away, like I had all the other times to protect myself. I took another deep breath and continued.

"I'm sorry if you feel threatened...by any of us on your care team."

He still hadn't blinked. My eyes watered.

"I'm even more sorry that you're in pain right now."

His right eyelid twitched, almost imperceptibly, at my sincerity.

I half whispered, like it was a poorly kept secret, "We just want to help you."

We sat in silence, just staring. After a small eternity, I withdrew from the ongoing smolder. I gently stood up, still saying nothing, and smoothed the front of my blouse. As I walked away, my diaper chafed the inside of my thighs. I crossed my arms to hide my hands, trembling with frustration and disappointment.

I'm done.

I was about to cross the threshold of the door when I heard a barely audible concession from behind me.

"I'll take 'em."

I met the widened eyes of his nurse. She had been patiently anticipating my failure in the hallway. I stepped aside, letting her pass by with his plastic cup of caplets.

On the other end of the hall, the attending poked her head out from the resident room—searching for me, presumably. I picked up my white coat and started jogging.

CHAPTER 7

SEMICOMA/STUPOR

SAM

The sentence was straight from my wildest dreams: "Sam, we need to go to the OR…now."

I swiftly spun my chair around to face Dennis, hovering in the doorway. Frantically, he motioned to follow before taking off toward the stairwell. My heart rate quickened.

This would be the part of the movie where Superman rips off his dress shirt to reveal his spandex suit. Time to save a life, suckas! It must be an emergency…maybe a head bleed?

"Time is brain. Right, boss?" Other Sam clapped my back as he jogged after the resident and left me in the workroom.

Ugh. It was his case. Other Sam was assigned to work with Dennis for the day.

How does this keep happening? He got every badass case this week—the brain tumor excisions, skull base surgeries, aneurysm clippings. I still haven't even seen a brain for crying out loud. He gets to scrub in for all the craniotomies while I assist with what? Carpal tunnel releases and battery replacements for spinal cord stimulators? How?

I returned to mindlessly scrolling through my patient notes; then my hip buzzed.

Dennis texted, *"Go into the other Sam's scheduled morning case instead. Way more interesting."*

Oh, thanks. Of course, Other Sam's scheduled case is more interesting. And I only get to move up the totem pole because that effer gets to go into an emergent procedure. I might as well take advantage.

"Will do! Thanks!"

As I went to pull up the OR schedule on my computer, I realized that Other Sam was still logged into his.

Bold, leaving up protected patient information. I could report him. Should I report him? Would he be exiled, and then I could assume my rightful place as The Only Sam?

Reaching over to grab his mouse—planning to sign him out like a virtuous citizen and never actually report him—I saw that his screen was filled with the OR schedule for next week as well as the residents assigned to each case.

What?

I clicked refresh five times to make sure I was seeing correctly.

How did he get this?

I knew how to find the OR schedule for the week—the procedures being performed, by what attendings, and at what times. Every common dingus knew how to find that, but the residents weren't listed on the schedule until the day of the surgery. Or so I thought. *Who knew there was a different way to view the schedule?*

Returning to my own screen, I madly adjusted a couple of settings, and sure enough, I could see the resident assignments, too.

That effer. Have I been royally sabotaged? Did he intentionally sabo me?

At the beginning of the week, Other Sam had asked if he could work with Dennis. He "really hit it off with him" on our first day, and "we could switch off next week so we'd both have opportunities to work with everyone." At the time, I thought, "What do I care?" I didn't know any of the residents yet, and switching off seemed fair.

But that effer had insider information. He knew Dennis had all the best cases this week while I got stuck doing battery changes with Logan. Next week, Logan has all the good stuff. Did Other Sam do this on purpose? Hard to believe this was unplanned...

I scrolled through the schedule again in disbelief.

Exhibit A: Dennis was originally supposed to be doing a spinal case this morning. Half of freaking neurosurgery is spine cases, and I still haven't seen a simple laminectomy.

My heart stopped when I saw the time.

Wait...

That's my case now! I played myself. I don't know anything about the spine! I've been preparing for my other cases...I haven't studied the spine at all. And the surgery starts in ten minutes!

I signed off both computers and sprinted to the OR. I managed to scrub in just in time for the attending to show up. Dr. Hayes was about a foot shorter than me and looked like a retired Marine—weathered and unamused with a high and tight haircut and big arms.

"Medical student?"

"How could you tell, sir?"

Why did I call him that?

He didn't laugh. As he looked me up and down, I realized there wouldn't be a resident on the case to protect me from his attention.

Damn it.

"Have you been on a spine case before?"

"No, sir."

There it is again. Come on, Sam, what is this, boot camp?

"Excellent, we can learn some stuff today."

That doesn't sound good. Am I about to get my shit rocked by this case?

I was, in fact, about to get my shit rocked. As soon as Sergeant Neurogod scrubbed in and returned to the patient's bedside, the pimping began.

"Let's say a patient gets stabbed in the neck and half of his spinal cord is transected. What's that called?"

It's happening. My first real pimping. Wait...I actually know this one.

"Brown-Séquard syndrome."

I distinctly remembered the question appearing on my Step 1 exam. *Moms would be so proud.*

"What are the deficits that occur on the same side as the injury?"

I pictured the textbook diagram in my head.

"Loss of proprioception, vibration, and two-point discrimination."

"And what about the other side?"

That must have been right, I guess...

"Loss of pain and temperature sensation one or two levels below the lesion."

"And why would that be on the other side?"

I realized how much I was sweating; my hands felt suffocated within two layers of gloves. *Thankfully his questions are straight out of the Step 1 board prep book.*

"Because the lateral spinothalamic tract nerve fibers cross over."

"What else?" he mused as he continued to work on exposing the patient's spine. I still hadn't been asked to help yet, so I just stood there across from him, kept my hands off the table, and prayed for mercy.

What else? Is he asking me or talking to himself, racking his brain for more pimp questions? Should I just start reciting information that I know? Give a mini lecture on neuroanatomy? Sing him the cranial nerve song that I made up?

Before I could say anything, he asked, "What spinal cord syndrome can be caused by occlusion of the anterior spinal artery?"

Softball question. Thank you, sir.

"Anterior cord syndrome."

I tried not to answer *too* quickly, as if I'd thought about it for a moment. *Maybe pimping won't actually be so bad? I'm crushing it.*

"What's a Jefferson's fracture?"

Spoke too soon.

I stayed silent as I flipped through imaginary textbook pages in my head.

Jefferson's fracture? When someone slips at Monticello and breaks their neck? Should I say that? Would he laugh?

He continued, "Do you know the difference between stable and unstable fractures?"

Is he not going to tell me what a Jefferson's fracture is? Stable versus unstable fractures...oh, I don't know, sir, one is freaking stable, and one isn't?

"Um, I guess...in stable fractures...the structural stability of the spine is intact..."

"Yes, that's the definition of stable."

"Right..."

I am never going to be a surgeon. I am spewing bullshit from my mouth all over this operating table. This is no longer a sterile environment. This is the end. It's over. If I drop out now, maybe I'll have time to enroll in a master's program that starts in the summer. That would be good. Maybe public health or something. Or perhaps I'll have to retire from public life permanently after this embarrassment. Unclear. We shall see.

At my silence, Dr. Hayes answered his own question: "Stable fractures occur in the anterior column of the spine. Unstable are midcolumn and posterior."

I nodded.

"Do you know what the atlas is?"

A map that my moms still keep in the back of their cars. Does he think I'm dumb now? Obviously, I know that one...

"The first cervical vertebrae."

He lifted his bloodied gloves to hold an imaginary globe in the air.

"Jefferson's fracture is a combined fracture of the anterior and posterior arches of the atlas. Very unstable. Think of Atlas, the Titan from the Greek myth, holding up the world with broken arms. Only this atlas holds up your head."

You know what's very unstable, sir? Me. My atlas is about to fracture carrying the weight of my medical school brain, and—apparently—I'm still an idiot anyway.

He positioned a retractor in the patient's back and said, "Here," handing it off to me.

Finally. I shyly stabilized my retractor arm with my free hand to keep it from shaking. *I need to start lifting weights.*

"What are the three types of dens fractures?"

I don't know, sir, I don't know anything! I would have reviewed this stuff if I knew I would be on a spine case today. Damn you, Other Sam!

"I don't know."

He took the retractor out of my hand.

"Look it up, and report on it during our next case together. I also want to know all the types of stable versus unstable cervical fractures. The names of them—clay-shoveler's, hangman's fracture, flexion teardrop."

What are these, heavy metal bands? He seems more like a classic rock/Americana kind of guy... He could be making these up, and I would be none the wiser.

"Yes, sir."

At the end of the six-hour case, the Pimp Captain dismissed me early for the day.

"Head home and study up, kid."

Shoot me, sir. Please just end me.

"Thank you!"

* * *

On my way home, power walking and panting, I texted Anna a stream of theatrics:

"Not gonna make it"
"Actively perishing"
"Total seppuku"
"This is the reckoning"
"Hello"

"Sorry, I had to Google seppuku. What is happening?"

"Pimped to extinction"
"Almost picked up scalpel to disembowel right then and there"
"At the feet of the pimp daddy himself"

"I hate that name."

"But that's what he is"

"You'll be okay. See you at home."

"Also, I'm starving."

"You'll be okay. See you at home."

I beat the other two to the house and promptly opened the neurosurgery e-book to its spine pages. An entire chapter covered "Types of Vertebral Fractures."

I read and re-read and carbon copied the whole section in my notebook. When my phone rang, I almost threw it through the kitchen window, especially when I saw that it was Moms.

Mama Dos was calling, but Mama B was probably there, too. They were always together when they called, which happened maybe every other full moon. I was usually the one phoning them for a weekly crisis. A lover of nicknames since childhood, I started calling them those names in kindergarten as a joke. With how competitive they were, I knew that they'd be offended thinking that the other was Mom #1 or Mom A in my mind. Somehow—probably just because it was clever, and I was adorable—the monikers stuck and evolved. Mom #2 became Mama Dos, and Mom B became Mama B.

What am I going to tell them? That their only son and next in line of the dynasty has to drop out of medical school because he doesn't know what a burst fracture is?

I took a deep breath. "Helloooo."

"How's our baby surgeon?" Mama B chirped.

"Sorry, ma'am, but I think you have the wrong number."

"Samuel." Mama Dos had less tolerance for my humor.

"I'm super-duper," I lied.

"Well, how the hell is it?"

"Well…"

"You know that if you chose neurosurgery, we would still love you."

Yea, that's definitely my concern right now… Not that I'm being sabo-ed by Other Sam, that I looked like King of the

Dingi with Sergeant Neurogod in the OR today, or that I feel like I still know diddly about surgery.

"I like it a lot! I just don't know if it's for me."

"Thank goodness. We can't stand neurosurgeons."

"Well, you don't have to worry, Moms." *About that...*

"Alright, go study, baby. Talk soon."

"Okay..."

Click.

Even though it had only been a week, I started questioning whether surgery was for me. I had always fantasized about standing in the OR—cutting and tying and cauterizing and suctioning—but then I had to actually *stand* in the OR.

Being on my feet for hours was exhausting. And the procedural stuff was cool, but my favorite parts of the rotation so far had been in clinic. I'm already tired. Why would anyone want to spend five years becoming a general surgeon and maybe even more to specialize after that? Heck, I'd be close to Dani's age by that point.

Speak of the devil, Dani banged on the window at that very moment, scaring the shit out of me. Anna was beside her. She opened the front door, and both of them barreled inside.

"Honey, we're home!" Anna sang.

"What a fucking day," Dani followed.

"Same, I'm naush."

"Naush?" Dani asked.

"He's nauseous," Anna translated.

Dani rolled her eyes and headed toward her room.

"Where are you going?" Anna exclaimed.

"I'll be right back, sweet girl!"

Anna took her seat at the table, pouting, and suggested that we get food delivered. Takeout was an uncommon luxury for us. Typically, Anna meticulously meal-prepped while Dani and I lived off pitiful prepackaged salads, freezer-burned Lean Cuisines, and protein shakes. After one long week on the wards—especially considering our interactions with Other Sam and Bitchy-Rachel—Anna and I concluded that we'd earned delivery. Plus, I was miserably anticipating scrubbing into my first craniotomy tomorrow.

"What's for dinner?" Dani reappeared, leaning against the doorframe.

Anna had already started laying out place settings, folding paper napkins so they stood up like pyramids on our mismatched plates, like we were about to experience fine dining instead of cheap takeout.

"I've only had a thimble of granola today, so we're treating ourselves to gastritis," I joked.

"We're ordering tacos," Anna clarified.

"Pick your poison." I offered Dani my phone with the menu pulled up, but she waved it away.

"I'd love to wreck my insides, but I have a date," she declared nonchalantly.

My jaw dropped, and I turned toward Anna, "Did you know about this?"

She nodded with a look of contempt.

"Loose Cannon, Dan, back at it…"

It's been eighty-four years since Dani went out with anyone. Her long-term relationship had abruptly come to an end a few months into medical school. She'd had a prolific dating life after that, but while we studied for boards the past couple of months, love was on hold (along with every other aspect of our existence). Dani going out on dates used to lead to many nights of Anna and I waiting up at the kitchen table for her.

Is that how it's going to be again? Is she going to abandon us when we will barely spend any time with each other this year anyway?

"Unbelievable."

"How many dates have you been on, and you've never, not once, taken me out to dinner?" Anna crossed her arms.

"Don't be dramatic, both of you."

Dani tousled her hair in the mirror next to the front door. *I guess she does look nice, but then again, she looks kind of like she always does...* She wore a black-ish sweater and black jeans. Her blonde hair was a mess, but in a good way, and she wore just a little bit of makeup, her "five-minute face," she called it.

She huffed before continuing, "I'm not really in the mood for this right now."

"Well, yeah, I mean why would you want to go spend time with a total stranger when you have two perfectly good best friends right here in the comfort of your own home?" Anna threw daggers.

"Don't listen to her, Dani. Your biological clock is ticking loud enough for all of us to hear. We get it."

She flipped me the middle finger with one hand and blew a kiss with the other on her way out the door.

Anna quipped, "So glad you didn't seppuku earlier or I'd be having dinner by myself. Tell me more about your session with pimp daddy."

"Oof, I had almost forgotten. Buckle up..."

CHAPTER 8

CHRONIC PAIN

—

DANI

*Eighty-one...eighty-two...*I'd lost count somewhere during my mid-twenties. And that was only *first* dates.

Maybe Anna has a point. Maybe I should focus on spending time with my friends—the people who already understand my life—instead of looking for love or companionship or whatever.

Or, even better, maybe I should focus on studying. Doctors weren't kidding when they said that medical school was like drinking from a fire hose. But wouldn't there always be more to learn? It won't stop during residency... When am I supposed to find a partner?

I snagged a parking spot one block south of the restaurant. Driving to dates was some version of an insurance policy: one drink, a two-hour parking limit, and a safe ride home. It wasn't my first rodeo, and I was acutely aware of the fact that I had to work the next day. Therefore, I had already chosen my entrée from the online menu and glanced at the admission notes for the new patient on the unit. My body sauntered into the trendy taqueria while my mind hovered back at the hospital.

The bar roared with end-of-the-workday excitement. Business-suited men and high-heeled women stood in clusters and talked over each other while sipping from Corona bottles. Bartenders chatted up seated customers while salt-rimming glasses and squeezing limes. Nostalgia punched me in the gut. *To be back on either side of that bar right now...enjoying happy hour on the company card or slinging drinks for a lively crowd instead of prerounding and progress notes...did I make a mistake?*

Plenty of men were waiting to be seated, but none were a match for my date's profile. *Meeting people on dating apps kind of sucks, but how else am I supposed to do it when I barely go out?* I prayed that I wasn't being catfished. Tonight's date was attractive and seemed like a successful business-type, hopefully not one to be intimidated by a medical student.

"James?"

I shouted his name toward the hostess, who searched for our reservation on a tablet.

"Party of two?"

I nodded.

"Is the other person in your party here yet?"

"I don't think so..." I glanced around before confessing, "First date."

"Ah," she smirked, "I'll put you at your table in the meantime, then."

The thunder of happy hour was quieter from the booth in the corner. A series of clocks bearing names of world cities lined the wall above James' empty seat. "It's five o'clock somewhere!" was painted in playful script on a plank of wood hanging above them.

Mr. Fruit Cup is due for his evening meds.

I replayed our encounter in my head.

"I'll take 'em."

What did I say that changed his mind? Would it last, or would things go back to normal tomorrow?

"Dani, I'm so sorry…"

James was better looking in person, a rare gift that distracted me from the fact that he was fifteen minutes late. A crisp white button-down shirt hugged his broad shoulders. His dark brown hair looked freshly cut and coiffed; streaks of amber glinted in it from the final hints of sunlight peeking in from the bar windows. Spirit danced in his fiercely blue eyes. I was intrigued.

"James!"

I stood up for our introduction and appreciated that he hugged me. *Just the right amount of pressure…comfortable hand positioning…an appropriate length of time…* James' hug was reassuring, demonstrating his comfort level with the situation and with himself.

"How was your day?" I started.

"Aw man, it was a rough one…I had this annual report to file—what do you do again? You're a nurse, right?"

"Medical student." I pretended not to be bothered by the gendered stereotype.

"What does that mean? Like, what are you going to be?"

"…a doctor…"

"Oh, wow! Very cool. What kind?"

"I don't know yet."

Why is this conversation already so exhausting? Probably because I've had it before…many times.

As James lost interest in the details of my career path, he started telling me about his "horrific" day at work. His comfort quickly unmasked itself as arrogance.

"…and you know, I make too much money to worry about that kind of thing when I show up for the day."

Here we go... I buckled up and waved down the waiter for a margarita. *Tell me about your terrible day at the office, James, please. Was the coffee maker broken? Was your inbox flooded?*

The bad days I'd had in my previous life were nothing compared to those in medical school, and I wouldn't expect him to understand. *I shouldn't be so harsh. Most people don't understand. I certainly didn't before I got to this point.*

James talked about himself for forty-seven minutes. I frequently glanced at the Cancún clock above his right shoulder and wondered if it was running slowly, but Barcelona off to his left confirmed the duration.

"Being the youngest manager in the office, there's a lot of pressure on me to work hard and play hard..."

"Women I've dated don't always seem to understand the demands of the job..."

"I don't even have the time to travel to check on my properties in LA and South Beach..."

"I was out until midnight last night partying with a client, but that's how you keep business, you know..."

I could easily interrupt, steer the conversation somewhere else, but I'm just...tired. I just want to get through this meal.

I cleared my plate before he even touched his. He noticed the discrepancy only after I moved my cloth napkin from my lap to the table. He grinned as he picked up one of his fish tacos, flashing remarkably sharp canines.

"Tell me something interesting about you."

I raised my eyebrows at him.

What is this, a medical school interview? Something interesting about me?

"Besides the fact that you're adorable."

Gross. Something interesting, hm...while you were partying last night, I was studying at my kitchen table. How's that?

He checked his phone to allow me time to prepare an acceptable response.

"And what kinds of things do you find interesting?" I sassed.

"Well, don't just try to impress me, now," he attempted at banter.

I have to get out of here.

"How about I impress you after we leave this restaurant?"

My intent to shock him was successful; genuine interest flashed across his face for the first time, and he slipped his phone back into his pocket. I let him pay the bill—it was the least he could do—as he revealed that he conveniently lived in the high-rise luxury apartment building right across the street.

"My place has a gorgeous balcony, and I can make a mean French 75. It's a classic cocktail," he mansplained as we walked out of the restaurant.

I know what a French 75 is. But you couldn't have known that because I didn't tell you I was a bartender. I didn't tell you anything about myself, actually.

"I just need to pop into this liquor store." He motioned to the hole-in-the-wall next door before wrapping his arm around the small of my back and pulling me toward him for a kiss. I grabbed his face like he was a dog that had eaten something off the sidewalk, clutching his mandible and stopping him two inches from my face.

I smiled. "Perfect. Why don't you run in, and I'll move my car."

He grinned stupidly as he walked away.

See you never.

Having every intention of driving away immediately, I climbed into the driver's seat.

What an asshole. At least it will be easy to drop him. Drop him... Ugh.

That rhetoric—"drop him," "forget him," "let him be someone else's problem"—was too familiar. *Didn't I just learn from Mr. Fruit Cup that the "let it be" strategy isn't the most effective? It won't change anything...*

I pulled up in front of the liquor store.

When James exited, carrying a bottle of Grey Goose, I rolled down the passenger side window.

He crouched over. "Couldn't find a spot?"

"I'm not coming in, actually," I stated calmly but firmly.

"Did something come up?" His furrowed brow somehow accentuated his jawline.

"Yes, I remembered that I had an appointment." I paused. "With my dignity, back at home."

"I don't understand."

"Tell me three things about me that you didn't know before our date," I challenged.

"Ha," he looked down the road and shook his head.

Unbelievable. "I hope you have the decency to treat your next date like a person. Show up on time. Ask them how their day was. Be respectful, listen. And one more thing for the record..."

I waited for him to return eye contact before I finished.

"There's no vodka in a French 75."

The stoplight turned green, and I pulled away, leaving James with his full liquor bottle and a flabbergasted expression on his face.

I should've stayed home with Sam and Anna. Or just gone to bed. What a colossal waste of time. If I'd been on this date before med school, I don't think I would've been that upset over it. Just another bad date. *Every minute of my time seems so much more precious now—I guess because it feels like I have so little of it.*

When I made it home, I was disappointed to find that the other two had already retired to their rooms. Stale fajita stink permeated the house, but Anna had ensured that the smell was the only lingering evidence of their meal.

I pulled a champagne flute off our home bar and polished it with a microfiber cloth. My collection of bar tools and glassware was one of the few physical remnants of my life before medical school. All of it was dusty.

Would I still be in my last relationship if I hadn't gone to med school? If I didn't have residency in front of me, would I be more relaxed about starting a new relationship? I'm not even sure if a relationship is what I need. Maybe I just need to feel something.

After packing a mixing glass with ice, I added an ounce of Tanqueray with practiced precision, followed by simple syrup of indeterminate age and juice from half a lemon, which was barely salvageable. I stirred the ingredients together noisily. I figured that my roommates couldn't be sleeping yet, and the sound might spark some curiosity, but no one appeared.

I strained the ingredients into the flute and popped a shitty bottle of sparkling wine to top it off. I rimmed the inside of the glass with a lemon twist that reminded me of my paper cut.

Maybe I should get used to this, being alone. After all, once I start gearing up for the exam at the end of this rotation, I'll fall off the grid again. Rinse and repeat for fourth year. Before, I loved my jobs. I can't say that I've really enjoyed med school. I used to make good money, too, and now I'm paying out of my ass to be here. All of my close friends are back on the other side of the country, which I haven't been able to visit since first semester. Not that it matters—most of them are busy planning weddings, buying homes, or having children. And here I am, with a sad cocktail and internal medicine flashcards.

Taking my seat at the kitchen table, I took a sip of my drink and pulled up study materials on my phone. *Might as well get through some of these. Only three thousand to review before the end of the block.*

An hour passed while I flipped through cards. After making a seemingly inconsequential dent in the deck, I poured the rest of my French 75 down the sink.

It's late, later than I thought. Did Mr. Fruit Cup take his overnight meds? I could sign in to check the medication log...

I eyed my backpack.

Why do I care so much? Why can't I accept that so much of this is out of my hands?

I lay awake until my alarm screeched.

* * *

Rubbing my eyes, I trudged into the hospital like a zombie. *I should have just slept here. That would have made my life so much easier.* When I reached my workstation, I opened Mr. Fruit Cup's medication log, and my eyes widened.

He had taken everything, even the late-night pills.

Smiling, I finished my usual preround routine then walked to the other end of the hall.

Mr. Fruit Cup was waiting for me when I knocked. He sat straight up in his bed with his hands folded neatly on his lap.

What is going on here?

Before I could greet him, he burst into tears.

What...

I reflexively grabbed a box of tissues and put my hand on his shoulder as I pulled a chair over next to his bed. He trembled at my touch but didn't push me away.

"Doctah Dani," he choked.

Student doctor, I mentally corrected him. *I don't think he's ever used my name before.*

After his third Kleenex, Mr. Fruit Cup told me about his PTSD. "The nightmares are awful. Just awful, Doctah Dani. And they come almost every night. They mostly about prison, about bein' assaulted. I can't even tell you what happen' to me. It's too awful. They came in at night, just like you people come in at night."

I felt a pang of guilt. *How could I have known?*

"Just awful. I was in there for somethin' dumb, too. Somethin' I regretted before it even happened. Then when I got out I was sleepin' on the streets. Well, not sleepin'." He shook his head at his bed sheets, "I don't think I slept for six years. I was paranoid. And the only thing that made me less paranoid was shootin' up. So, I shot up."

I stayed quiet but nodded in acknowledgement. He went on, "At first, it was only a couple times a week. To take the edge off. To get me to the next day. But you know how that shit works." His words were heavy with grief and regret.

All that…reduced to "previously incarcerated" and "history of IV drug abuse" in his chart.

"Sometimes I even wake up kickin' and screamin'. But from other dreams, worse ones. So much worse. Three years ago, it was the worst day of my life, and I had a lot of bad days. She…" He paused and sobbed for a moment.

Why is he telling me this?

"She wasn't breathin' no more. I rolled over and my wife was there next to me, where she always was. She wasn't even sick. She never did drugs a day in her life. Never even tried 'em. Just me. I tried to get clean for her. So many times, I tried to get clean, but I kept slippin'. And then she slipped away." He sniffled once and clenched his fist full of dirty tissues. "They said it was an aneurysm."

I felt my heart break in my chest. I still hadn't spoken a word when his gaze locked with mine, and he confessed: "I ain't told that to nobody."

When he dabbed the last tears from his eyes, glowing softly, he muttered, "You can listen to my heart now."

CHAPTER 9

ABDOMINAL PAIN

SAM

Woof. Okay. Just a craniotomy. Just a brain. Just a human brain, hanging out in some guy's open skull while we fix it. Well, while they *fix it. Not a big deal. Has anything in my life, any single thing, made me feel as inadequate as I do right now, standing here in the shadow of a neurosurgeon? Probably not. I can't think of anything. I can't think at all, really.*

"Nick, can you clip him?" Dr. Lee addressed me.

Ah, my name is Nick now. Close enough. I might just have to change it legally. I like the name—good, strong, monosyllabic. Classic, Nick is. Okay, "Nick," use your words.

"Sure! That's within my skill set."

The nurse laughed, and I liked her immediately. The surgeon was simply asking me to shave the patient's head, to prepare the area where he'd be working. Not to clip the aneurysm that brought the patient to the OR. I can't tell if he smiled at my joke under his surgical mask or not, but I had to pretend. The nurse handed me the clippers.

I inspected the patient's head and quickly realized I had lied. This was not actually within my skill set. I had questions.

How much do I shave? Do I totally "Mr. Clean" this guy? Do I give him a hemi-trim, up-and-down like a lawnmower on just the one side? Drag the vibrating blade in a circle around his parietal lobe? Or maybe "X" marks the spot, like on a treasure map, right over the aneurysm?

I went with the safe option: to slowly and carefully bumble in a tiny area until the resident took pity on me, placed her hand over mine, and guided a few strokes over the rest of the patient's globe. She had only six years of training under her belt so, presumably, she knew how to operate the clippers. Thankfully, my face mask hid both my horrific embarrassment and the spicy chorizo lingering on my breath.

My stomach churned, reminding me of last night's feast. Anna and I had overdone it. We demolished a family platter consisting of tacos, enchiladas, quesadillas, fajitas, and nachos meant to feed no fewer than four people. She'd said, "no regrets," as she kicked her feet up onto Dani's empty chair. I echoed, "no regrets," while releasing the top button of my jeans and patting my bloated gut.

"Nick, why don't you go scrub in? Do a full ten minutes."

Ten minutes? The neurosurgeon went back to flirting with the OR staff before I could get clarification. They ate up every single word that came out of his mouth. The lot of them giggled while they bent over backward to prepare his stage precisely the way he liked it. *I guess he is handsome? He has the whole silver fox thing going on and walks around like he owns the place. But a ten-minute scrub?*

Handsome Neurosurgeon must have thought that medical students were dirtier than the average OR personnel. I hadn't heard of any evidence that scrubbing for more than five minutes had any additional efficacy for preventing infection. Surely, the neurosurgery gods knew this. But I complied.

At the hallway sink, I adjusted my face mask and scrub cap in the reflection of the metal paper towel dispenser. I didn't recognize myself. I stepped on the floor pedal to start the water, letting it run over my hands and forearms. I used the sterile plastic pick to scrape underneath my fingernails, bitten down to nubs. I dragged the flexible bristles of one side of the scrub brush over my ragged cuticles, then flipped it over and used the yellow sponge side to create a pinkish foam. I scrubbed every surface of every finger on my left hand before moving to the palm, sides, and back of the hand, then down and around my forearm, then over to the right-hand side. I watched the clock. Six minutes had passed—only six.

I continued scrubbing until my skin felt raw and foam fell from my elbows in large globules. When ten painfully slow minutes had elapsed, I rinsed off the last of my invisible filth. I pushed open the door to the OR with my hip, holding my dripping arms in a boxing stance to not bump into anything and "break scrub." I smiled enthusiastically, knowing full well that no one could see and that no one cared anyway. The scrub tech, already sterile, handed me a blue surgical towel to pat myself dry, then helped me into a stiff fabric gown, the first set of latex gloves, and then the second set.

Handsome Neurosurgeon and the resident already stood at the patient's head, and I took my place somewhat off to the side. The resident picked up the scalpel, and I felt my stomach churn again. My intestines began twisting themselves into knots. They screamed audibly during the initial incision as if they were being sliced open instead of this patient's scalp. The resident looked up as if to silence me with her eyes.

Shut up, shut up, shut up.

The resident created a flap, folding back a layer of skin and muscle to reveal the glistening cranium. It was beautiful.

She and Handsome Neurosurgeon exchanged words, which I pretended to hear as my gut twist progressed to outright writhing. The surgical drill's shrill sound drowned out the shrieks from the depths of my abdomen. I became very aware of the burbling under my surgical gown.

How is this happening to me right now? Do I excuse myself? I said a prayer to the neurosurgery gods that the hot trickle down the back of my leg was, in fact, sweat.

"Be strong," I mentally whispered to my sphincters.

The drilling paused.

"You okay? It's okay if you need to step out."

The resident must have noticed that all color had drained from my face.

Damn it. She thinks I'm queasy because of the procedure. They think that I am weak, that the sight of metal grinding against skull or the smell of bone dust in the air caused me to decompensate when it was actually a pint of queso.

"Thank you," I heard myself whimper as I slowly and calmly stepped back from the table. As quietly as possible, I peeled off my gown and gloves, then tiptoed to the door. I opened it narrowly and squeezed through as if I were sneaking out instead of being watched by every pair of eyes in the room (besides those of the patient with the open head). At the click of the doorknob, I began a full sprint to the only single stall on the unit.

I barely got my pants to my ankles in time. The harsh light reflected off my pasty thighs as I epically relieved myself. Sweat drenched the pits of my arms and knees, darkening the blue of my scrubs. I ripped off my face mask and dabbed the perspiration from my brow. I texted Anna, *"I have regrets."*

I pulled myself together. Really, I did. I splashed cold water on my face, changed my scrubs, and replaced my cap and face mask. I paced up and down the locker room, mustering the courage to reenter the OR. I had to. I was a medical student. I was to continue the surgical dynasty. I was a victim of the family taco platter. A survivor, one might say.

I returned to the scrub sink. Ten minutes seemed warranted this time. I shuffled back into the OR like a puppy with its tail between its legs. The scrub tech graciously helped me redry, regown, and reglove.

"Feeling better?" asked Handsome Neurosurgeon, not looking up from his work. He stood where the resident had. Together, they had finished creating a bone flap by sawing an oval into the skull. He traced the edges with his gloved fingertips, then slipped one underneath the fragment to pry it away. He gently peeled it back, separating it from the dura mater—the tough, fibrous outer membrane surrounding the brain.

"Much better, thanks," I mumbled as I resumed my place in his shadow.

He pinched the membrane with forceps and lifted it gently. Using a scalpel with the other hand, he created an incision to reveal a majestic, living, pulsating, gray-pink human brain. It looked so different than it had in the cadaver lab, where it was more of a shriveled, dense, putty-colored specimen. He held the membrane there for a moment like a tiny tent pitched over the most complex organ of the human body. My intestines squealed. Again.

Why? Why?

I stood completely still.

I'm about to desecrate this OR.

I didn't wait for the resident to notice this time. I didn't tiptoe. I didn't creep. I took off like an underdog thoroughbred at the Kentucky Derby when the bell sounds and stall doors bust open. Maybe I looked like I was running to a code or something important as I raced down the hallway to my single stall. I thanked the neurosurgery gods that the throne of despair was still available.

That was that. I couldn't scrub again. I couldn't scrub *thrice*. I knew what I had to do: three things.

First, I texted the resident, letting her know that I was experiencing food poisoning and that I would loiter in the lounge until the procedure was finished. That I was happy to help with any other tasks for the day. That I was mortally embarrassed and extremely sorry.

Second, I looked at the schedule for the rest of the week. I made sure I was slated to be anywhere but in Handsome Neurosurgeon's OR so that I would never see him again.

Third, I left a scathing Yelp review of the family taco platter. Anonymous, of course.

CHAPTER 10

FAILURE TO THRIVE

ANNA

Fwack! My innocent cell phone faceplanted on the hardwood as I feverishly flung my sheets to my feet. When my alarm went off, my fingers had caressed "stop" instead of "snooze" in a state of hospital-induced delirium. I clocked myself at roughly twenty-three minutes behind schedule, slapped on my scrubs, and haphazardly dabbed concealer over my exhaustion.

Everything's fine...

I patted myself on the back—making record time from deep sleep to driver's seat—then missed my highway exit. By no small miracle and no major traffic violations, my tires screeched into the employee garage with time to spare. The hurried *squeak-squish-squeak-squish* of my plastic hospital clogs on the waxed linoleum hesitated only when my keys fell from the pocket of my pressed white coat.

"You're kind of late today, huh?" Bitchy-Rachel handed me a patient chart as thick as the Holy Bible when I walked into the resident room.

I glanced up at the clock, branded with a stork in flight and a baby in tow between five and six. I was still ten minutes early. *I'm later than usual, but not for my shift. She knows that. I beat most of the residents here every day.*

"I'm sorry," I offered halfheartedly.

Ugh, why am I apologizing? I wasn't late!

"There's not much going on this morning. Nights have been horrific lately, just nonstop deliveries, so there are no active laborers on the floor right now." She announced this as though she had single-handedly managed the evening cases instead of showing up for morning handoff like the rest of the day team. She nodded toward the chart in my hand.

"There was a complicated delivery a couple of months ago, a joint case with pediatrics that we're talking about during Grand Rounds next week. Read through the chart, and go down to the NICU in an hour to see the baby with the peds team."

Twenty questions popped into my head all at once, but Bitchy-Rachel had already waddled her pregnant belly out of the room.

So, I'm supposed to sit here for an hour and peruse this chart? Do I go to morning sign-out? Is she just pawning me off to the peds team today, so she doesn't have to deal with me? Where is the neonatal ICU?

I answered most of my own questions, as usual. The paper chart was more of a decoy than anything else, containing only outside records already scanned into the EMR. All the relevant progress notes were in the system, and the baby was not actually in the NICU but on another peds floor. From what I gathered, a lot of social issues surrounded the case, and Mom had a high-risk pregnancy. The baby was born with a heart defect, leaving him oxygen dependent until it could be repaired.

The pediatrics team had updated the baby's most recent note only minutes before: "JJ is status quo. Down to two liters overnight but then desatted to the low eighties. Today, back up to four liters. Follow q4h vitals. Wean O2 as tolerated."

As I read, the silence of the resident room struck me. *Where is everyone? Am I missing something?* After I skimmed through half a million documents, the stork clock declared that I had just enough time to grab a bite from the cafeteria before looking for JJ.

I snatched up a granola bar from the grab-and-go station and was thrilled to find only one person ahead of me in the check-out line. *I probably won't have enough time to use the restroom, though.* As I swiped my card to pay, a familiar voice carried over from the dining area.

Bitchy-Rachel, seated at the head of the table, was passing out hot fresh donuts to the rest of the day team. The other residents were joking with one another, laughing and throwing playful elbows. Bitchy-Rachel wasn't smiling, but she seemed to be the leader of the activity.

My heart sank. *Was I sent on a fool's errand? Was I made to read through that ridiculous chart so that I wouldn't ruin their breakfast? Will I ever feel like part of the team as a medical student?* I tucked my meager breakfast into my pocket and left the cafeteria, no longer hungry.

Outside of JJ's room, the medical students on pediatrics informed me that we were about to engage in a wildly uncomfortable exercise known as "physical diagnosis rounds." This medical student privilege was akin to a field trip to the zoo, an opportunity to gather 'round a unique creature to poke, prod, and observe. Firsthand exposure to distinctive physical exam findings would presumably make us more likely to recognize them during future clinical encounters.

A new inhabitant of both the pediatric intermediate care unit and the cruel, cruel world, forty-two-day-old JJ peered at us through the rungs of his enclosure. The whole flock of us, donning yellow masks and gowns, took turns listening to the rhythmic *click-whoosh* murmur that kept JJ in the hospital.

"What are the four cardiac defects associated with Tetralogy of Fallot?" began today's round of *Jeopardy!*, hosted by our resident tour guide.

I didn't raise my hand but answered correctly in my head. *Why do I never speak up?*

The room felt sterile, without any warmth of a typical nursery. The tall white crib was centered to the back wall of the room, painted canary yellow to match our gowns. A lonely gray armchair sat beside it. Not a single stuffed animal, balloon, or toy was in sight. *Well, this is depressing.*

Swaddled in a tiny blanket with baby blue elephants marching across it, JJ looked more like a fresh newborn than a six-weeker. His bright orange cap, probably hand-knit by a hospital volunteer, would barely fit over a grapefruit. The little pumpkin wore a plastic oxygen mask that covered most of his tiny face. It quietly hissed as his chest moved up and down.

The loud rips of shedding gowns signaled the end of the medical student interrogation. As our flock paraded out the door, I asked the resident why the room was so empty. A pained cringe and prolonged pause preceded his response: "JJ has had some family issues, maybe a question of abuse. He's alone."

My heart ached as I recalled from JJ's chart that, on top of his heart defect, he had initially presented with failure to thrive, having lost twenty percent of his birth weight.

Failure to thrive. Who named that diagnosis? Don't we all experience "failure to thrive" at some point?

The resident perked up as he added, "Volunteers come by to hold him during the day; if you ever have some time, feel free to pop in!"

I wish volunteers would hold me during the day.

I trudged back to the labor and delivery workroom and found it empty. Contempt flooded my consciousness.

Maybe the day team went out for an early lunch.

I texted the entire group: "Hey! Done with peds rounds and back in the resident room. Please let me know where I can help."

I slowly spun around in a computer chair while nibbling on my granola bar. The stork clock ticked loudly—I hadn't noticed this annoyance before—while I checked and rechecked the tracking board for any new patients. Cracking open a dusty textbook that permanently lived in the workroom, I read up on prenatal infections, third trimester bleeding, and postpartum hemorrhage. I had just started the chapter on eclampsia management when Bitchy-Rachel stormed in.

"Oh, hi," she greeted me with audible disinterest. She almost looked surprised to see me there, exactly where I was supposed to be.

"Anything I can help with this afternoon?" *Thanks for answering my text.*

"Check back in a couple of hours," she flatly instructed as she sat at her computer station, facing away from me.

A couple of hours? What am I supposed to do for a couple of hours? Being here right now has approximately zero educational value for me, and my time is important. Why wouldn't you just send me home? You know I'm switching to the night shift. Is it so hard to remember what it's like to be a medical student?

"Sounds good."

I didn't want to be there, in that room with just the two of us, any more than she did.

If I have a couple of hours to burn, I might as well be holding a baby.

After shyly notifying JJ's nurse of my intentions, I crept to his crib side. He lay awake, sucking on a green pacifier underneath his oxygen mask and staring attentively at the ceiling. I scooped him up, careful not to disrupt the mess of wires connecting him to the wall.

The armchair's fake leather squealed beneath me as I tried to get comfortable. Aside from the occasional beep from his monitor, JJ's room was painfully quiet. *Should I talk to him?* He blinked up at me, helpless and pitiful and beautiful and perfect.

"Hey, little guy."

I lightly rocked us back and forth in the chair.

"I know it's hard to be alone."

His pacifier bobbed up and down as he listened. I spoke softly.

"Even if you're not alone all the time, sometimes it feels like it. Especially when you don't know where you are or where you're supposed to be."

He squirmed, wriggling inside his swaddle. I stood up and walked us in a semicircle around his crib, as far as the wires would allow.

"It'll get better, buddy."

Would it? I shouldn't have promised him that. I hoped it would get better. I should stop talking.

"Let's put on some music."

Gently resting JJ back in his crib for a moment, I visited the computer at his bedside and pulled up a "feel good" playlist. A light and whimsical tune—"All Day All Night," an indie pop/rock song by Moon Taxi—filled the formerly stale room. Plucking JJ up from his bed again, I resumed our feeble waltz.

His pacifier seemed to bounce more vigorously with every step. He startled me when he kicked his tiny bare foot out of his swaddle; that seemed to bounce, too.

I paused. He was dancing.

Would ya look at that...

His monitor was still beeping—out of sync with the song—and, from the corner of my eye, I saw flashing red numbers turn steadfast green. His oxygen saturation was going up.

We kept dancing, twirling forward and backward, shuffling and sliding across the floor. I forgot all about my terrible morning, my crippling exhaustion, and Bitchy-Rachel. I watched and waited for JJ's numbers to dip back to the scarlet-hued eighties.

They didn't.

When my arms got tired and I returned JJ to his crib, his tracking chart boasted its best pulse oximeter tracings since his admission. I set the playlist to continue on an endless loop and added a communication note to the chart, hoping it would reach any future volunteers: "JJ loves to dance. Please play music during your visit."

I returned to the resident room after a couple hours had passed, as instructed. Bitchy-Rachel was alone in her usual spot, scrolling through an operative report.

I cleared my throat to announce myself and started to ask, "Is there anything that—"

"No," she cut me off and curtly dismissed me for the day: "You can go home." Her eyes remained glued to her computer screen.

What a blessing.

"Thanks, have a good one."

I happily bounced out of the hospital, humming.

CHAPTER 11

WEAKNESS

DANI

What day is it? That mid-week sucker punch hit me as I watched the dreaded spinning wheel on my desktop screen. Being at the hospital every day was like a time warp of tedium. I'd been so exhausted trying to balance studying for Shelf, reading for work, and basic activities of daily living—but it felt like I was making no progress.

Well, my relationship with Mr. Fruit Cup was the one exception.

After his revelation over the weekend, things were turning around. For me, at least. He was still pretty impossible for most other hospital staff, but now, they went looking for me if he gave anyone a hard time. He started opening up to a couple others—the phlebotomist who talked sports with him and the evening nurse who brought him tea. He was still refusing physical therapy, though. I read the PT notes, and it sounded like he gave them hell. I wasn't looking forward to asking him about it.

I knocked and heard, "Guh'mornin', Doctah Dani!" before I even entered.

"Good morning! How are you feeling today?"

"Surer than shit," his voice carried a note of surprise, "I'm a feelin' alright."

"That's what I like to hear! What happened with physical therapy yesterday?"

His face quickly turned grim, and he shook his head.

"You know…that lady comes in here. Every. Damn. Day." He slapped his thigh with each word. "She'll be smilin' and jokin' when I'm in no jokin' mood. So I say, 'Noooo ma'am. Git out.'"

That sounded familiar.

"Why are you in no joking mood?"

"Doctah Dani," he tone switched to matter-of-fact. "You shoulda seen me when I was a young man. I looked like one of them."

He pointed to the football players on the television screen.

"I could lift two hundred pounds and had a belly like a washboard. You betta belie'me."

It was hard to believe, considering the waif of a man in front of me. His weight hadn't come up despite the daily Ensure shakes on top of regular meals.

"Boxin' was my sport. I loved every sport, though. I still love 'em all. Boxin' was the most useful though, and I use'ta make money from it."

"Make money from it?" I sat down in the chair next to his bed, genuinely curious and accepting that our morning chat would take at least a good fifteen minutes.

"I use'ta fight down at the south side gym in tourna-mitts, big tournamitts. My name on the postahs and everythin'." He looked up and waved his hands with his fingers fanned out in front of his face. "I could make fifty dollahs, a hundred sometimes, in a few fights in a single weeken'. And that's where I met my wife."

He turned squarely toward me. "Doctah Dani—you gotta man?"

I opened my mouth and laughed awkwardly. I hated that question, even if I was dating a man when it was asked. That was the best-case scenario—to check the box that was expected, which would avoid further questioning or, worse, unwanted advances. Otherwise, I could be dating a woman, in which case it usually became awkward for everyone. *Where is this going?*

"Don't really mattah, I guess. Whether you do or whether you don't. Because I betcha you lost somebody before. Everybody's lost somebody some time. And that hurts like nothin' else in the whole world—except losin' yourself."

Leaning forward, he rubbed both of his knobby knees through his blanket. His voice quieted. "That physical therapist came in here in a jokin' mood, and the fact that I can barely walk to the bathroom is no joke to me. I used to be able to do anythin'. I used to run a few miles every damn day. But I lost myself." He bit the inside of his cheek as he ran his hands up his skinny thighs.

"You ever think maybe somebody could help you find yourself?"

Shaking his head, he muttered, "I don't trust *nobody*."

Neither do I.

"I wouldn't either after all you've been through. But if you're going to be here anyway, maybe we can at least try to get you steady on your feet."

He raised his eyebrows. "What, you mean you're going to walk with me?"

"Well…if and when the physical therapist clears you for it…I'll go for a walk up and down this unit with you every damn day."

Matching his language earned me a smirk.

"Deal."

"So if I call PT, you'll let them evaluate you today?"

"Yes, ma'am."

"Alright. Can I get you anything else?"

"Uh, yes, actually—can I please get a fruit cup with my breakfast?"

"I'm going to start calling you Mr. Fruit Cup." *Little does he know...*

"Ha!" His outburst startled me. He clapped his hands together once. "I like it. Mistah Fruit Cup."

I let out a sigh of relief as I left his room. *I shouldn't have said that...I still need to tread lightly.*

When I returned and handed him his diced peaches, he loosely gripped the sleeve of my coat.

I stiffened up, remembering Jay's early warning not to get too close.

"Thank you," he earnestly stated, "Doctah Dani."

"Student doctor," I corrected him.

"No, no." He shook his head. "*You*—you're my doctah."

I gloated in his chart, "After discussion, the patient is amenable to physical therapy."

* * *

Later at the kitchen table, I ate dinner alone and studied in silence, waiting for Sam to get home.

When he finally made his entrance, he dropped his keys on the floor and almost knocked his glasses off his face. Looking around the kitchen with confusion, he asked, "Where is sweet girl?"

"Hm, nice to see you, too."

He probably wanted to talk shop and knew I didn't tolerate that as much as Anna did. I didn't care who was studying already and how much, who scored what on which practice tests, or how Reddit decoded the key to succeeding on Shelf.

"Sorry, I'm a POS." [Translation: Piece of shit.] "But actually, where is she? She's not answering my texts."

"She's on nights this week. You knew that."

"Ugh, lame." He took his seat and started his usual tap dance, bouncing his restless legs. "How was the date, wench?"

"Wow, I had just about forgotten it."

"That good, huh? Come on, hit me with it…"

I straightened my back and presented my date like I would a patient on rounds. "Thirty-three-year-old male 'consultant' presents fifteen minutes late to dinner because he was 'having a stressful week.' Endorses fatigue and irritability. Denies working past six p.m., skipping meals, or being on his feet for more than five minutes at a time. Demands that I tell him something interesting about myself while intermittently checking his phone."

Sam didn't blink. "Did you murder him?"

I chuckled, and he pressed for the next section of my presentation: "Physical exam?"

"Unremarkable."

"Oof."

"Just kidding," I huffed. "Annoyingly handsome. Medium-build, blue eyes, well-groomed…"

"Assessment and plan?" Sam cut me off, wanting the abbreviated version.

"Dispo home with no follow-up."

"Onto the next sucka?"

"I suppose," I sighed.

"You got this, bud."

He knew that I was upset, but he didn't know what to say; that was okay. He would listen if I wanted to talk about it. I was just glad he didn't remind me, "You know Moms didn't meet until fellowship."

Sure, it was reassuring to know that some people find love later. But how do you tell your best friend that you just don't feel like yourself anymore? All of the things that brought me joy, that defined me—reading and writing, getting to know people from behind the bar, my relationship—I abandoned at the start of med school. What was left?

I turned the conversation back to him. "How was the OR today?"

"Worse than your date. I would much rather be wined and dined by an asshat than scrub into another surgery."

"Do Moms know that you're going to be a pediatrician yet?"

"Watch your mouth."

"You got this, bud!" I mimicked playfully.

He sighed dramatically as he stood up and slung his backpack over his shoulder. "I'm not sure that I do."

"I'm not sure that I do either," I kicked his leg gently from my seat, "but we're in it together."

He nodded at the floor.

"If you need anything, you know where I live."

"Thanks, dingus."

As Sam shuffled to his room to study for the night, I sipped my evening coffee and traced the watermarks on the tabletop with my thumb. *Does every med student feel like this? Will I continue to be a shell of myself after matching into residency? After I'm an attending?*

Mr. Fruit Cup's words replayed in my head: *"And that hurts like nothing else in the whole world—except losing yourself."*

CHAPTER 12

HYPOCHONDRIASIS

SAM

I am not a hypochondriac. This is a legitimate concern. I am not a hypochondriac.

As a renowned neurosurgeon lectured an auditorium of esteemed medical professionals, I repeatedly pressed my fingers into my neck. A kidney bean-sized lymph node sat underneath my jawline on the right side. I couldn't tell if it was tender. Though, any part of my body would be tender if prodded incessantly—like I had been doing to my neck for twenty minutes—so it was hard to say.

How long has it been like that? Days? Weeks? Months? How have I not noticed it before?

"Well, it's not rocket science..."

The lecturer made a joke about how easy it was to be a neurosurgeon, and the audience of neurosurgeons cackled.

Assholes. I'm barely holding on during the second week of my rotation. Sleep was a foreign concept. Human interaction was minimal. My outlook was bleak. *And* I was having a health crisis.

Running through the pertinent positives and negatives of my medical history, I began building a differential for my enlarged lymph node. *It could be a tumor or infection or some other sort of inflammation—or a tumor. Do I have lymphoma? Did I have any B symptoms...think...any systemic symptoms at all? Fever, night sweats...I'm always sweating...*

I discreetly pulled out my phone and searched for "lymphoma" on one of my thirty medical apps. The age range fit. Painless neck lump. Unilateral. *Maybe* nontender.

I could have lymphoma.

Discreetly text spamming Anna was the next logical move:

"*I need you to feel this lymph node when I get home*"
"*Cervical lymph node*"
"*Unilateral*"
"*Can't tell if it's tender or not*"
"*Doesn't feel right*"
"*Should I make an appointment?*"

Shoot. I remembered that she was on night shift. She was probably sleeping and wouldn't answer me. Therefore, copying and pasting my initial message to send to Dani was the *next* logical move.

"*I need you to feel this lymph node when I get home*"

Flipping over my phone in my lap, I glanced around the auditorium to see if anyone had noticed that I wasn't paying attention. No one was looking—which was not shocking, considering that I was tucked in the back corner of the moderately-sized amphitheater—but my paranoia persisted. The real doctors could still see me from their sections if they *really* wanted to.

The room's hierarchical seating arrangement was obvious. Attendings and special guests sat on the far side of the auditorium, as far away as possible from the medical students. They blithely sipped their coffees and seemed to be listening intently, maybe even *enjoying* the presentation. Residents occupied the middle section. They were a mildly disheveled bunch, furtively peeking at their pagers between fits of aggressive nodding at the speaker to demonstrate that they were, in fact, paying attention, despite the ongoing demands of patient care. Medical students sat on the other side, completely in the dark. Literally—the entire panel of lights was out above our section. It was unclear whether there was an electric problem or if concealing us was intentional.

Considering the interdisciplinary nature of the late afternoon talk, some of the medical students on neurology and general surgery rotations were seated in the rows in front of me. *Where is Other Sam? I don't think there's a case going on right now. Is he skipping?* No hiding places were apparent. Even if he somehow infiltrated another section, I could see every seat in the auditorium and couldn't locate his perfectly coiffed hair.

People started clapping, so I started clapping, marking the end of the lecture. I inhaled a stairwell granola bar on my way back to the resident room, and Dani finally responded to my node exam request: *"Jesus Christ. Okay."*

Other Sam walked into the workroom a second behind me. *Where was the Sabotage King during the presentation?*

The intern, who was completely swamped returning never-ending pages, had a legitimate excuse for not being there. He weakly smiled at the two of us while holding the desk phone to his ear. His bloodshot eyes were somewhat frightening. "Hey guys, what was the lecture topic?"

"Hydrocephalus and shunts," Other Sam answered before me.

My head snapped in his direction. *You weren't even there!*

"Cool. Who gave the talk?"

Returning my gaze, Other Sam raised his eyebrows and confirmed my suspicion. He definitely wasn't there.

"Dr. Rosario," I declared.

"Aw man, she's the best. Hopefully you guys'll get to work with her while you're here."

Other Sam chimed back in, "Yeah, she's awesome! She's also from North Carolina. We figured that out during one of our cases together. We grew up in the same area."

This freaking gunner... He probably looked that up online before he went into the case and made sure that it came up.

The intern continued the small talk as he multitasked: "Do you guys know what you want to go into?"

"I think I'm interested in surgery, but I'm not sure yet. I'm trying to keep an open mind as I go through rotations," I confessed with rehearsed sincerity.

Other Sam replied, "I'm really thinking neurosurgery, actually. I did research with spinal cord devices in undergrad."

"No way!" The intern stopped what he was doing to listen to Other Sam.

"Yeah, I worked with the same manufacturer of the device that we put in our patient this morning."

I was gagging internally when Dennis walked in and added, "Sam, that was awesome that you knew how to program the stimulator earlier! Really good work today."

Yeah, Sam, excellent work today. What did you think of the hydrocephalus lecture? Did you like the part about the... mmm...okay, maybe I wasn't paying attention, but at least I was there.

After glancing at his watch, Dennis told us both that we should leave for the day, which was music to my ears. I'd be able to get a head start on my studying for the night, maybe even take an extended dinner break.

"Oh, also! I have your midcourse feedback forms. Take them before I lose them. We can talk through them tomorrow if you want."

Dennis handed us each an envelope, which I promptly tucked into my backpack. After logging off my computer and grabbing my coat, I lingered in the doorway—as was the polite thing to do—to walk out with Other Sam.

"Don't wait up. I need to print a couple of things, and then I'll be right behind ya!"

Hmph. I guess I won't have the opportunity to interrogate you regarding your whereabouts during the conference. Where could you possibly have gone? Outside to the patio to enjoy a nice lunch break? To the library to study? Am I doing this wrong? Other students attended the lecture, so I can't be the only one following the rules.

When I reached the crosswalk to the employee garage, I realized I had left my favorite water bottle at the computer station again. Jingling my keys around in my pocket, I kept walking. *It'll be fine...right? It'll still be there in the morning when I get back. The overnight team will hang around in that room, maybe? Ugh, I should get it.*

I dragged my feet back over the crosswalk, through the side entrance, and down the hall. As I was about to reach the stairwell, Other Sam and Dr. Rosario walked out in front of me, appearing to be deep in conversation. They didn't notice me and turned away to walk toward the OR. Other Sam talked animatedly with his hands, and Dr. Rosario laughed, patting him on the back.

Did he know we had an add-on case? I didn't even think to look. What am I saying? Of course, he knew. He is the Sabotage King and Gunner-in-Chief. I hope she asks him about her presentation.

Boiling hot, I made my way to the resident room only to discover that my water bottle wasn't there.

"What the literal *heck*?"

Craning my neck, I looked behind every computer screen. I just about got on my knees to look under the table. I even rifled through some papers as if they could be obscuring the thirty-two-ounce container.

Where is it? Moms got me that on our last family vacation. I've had it for ten years. Where the eff could it be?

"Whatcha looking for?" Dennis' eyebrows were raised in concern, or maybe alarm.

"My water bottle. It's a blue Nalgene. It has a Lake Tahoe sticker on it…"

"Um…" Dennis paused. "Like the one in your backpack?"

I reached behind me to pat the side of my bag. My water bottle was tucked neatly there, exactly where it was supposed to be. And, unnecessarily, Dennis just witnessed me have a minor hysterical fit. "Yep!" I fake chuckled. "That would be the one. Disregard."

Damn it, Sam. And damn you, Other Sam. Ugh.

On my way home, I attempted some deep-breathing exercises and tried not to throw up. Pacing back and forth in the kitchen usually helped, so I tried a bit of that too when I arrived. My pulse and respiratory rate were normalizing when I remembered the envelope containing my mid-course feedback.

The flap was simply tucked in, not actually sealed, but I ripped it anyway. After unfolding the evaluation sheet, I scanned it up and down about fifty times. I flipped it over, already knowing that the back page was blank, then over again, hoping different feedback might magically appear.

I got three-bombed.

Multiple rows with titles like "history taking," "physical exam," and "oral presentations," among others, were labeled with scales from one to five. My entire sheet—the whole sheet—was filled with bubbles right down the middle. Three out of five, in every single category.

How! *How does this happen? How can I be a surgeon if I'm only average? Forget matching at a top ten program for anything, never mind surgery. This isn't going to fly. I'll need honors across the board in every rotation. Getting honors isn't even supposed to be* that *hard. Basically, a third of students get honors with all the grade inflation...*

I just about exploded when Dani walked through the door. "*Dani!*"

Dani shook her head. "Sam, I'm sure the lymph node is fine..."

"Oh my *god*, I forgot about the node. This is worse..."

"Please hold," she said assertively and raised her hand as if she were stopping traffic. I held my breath as she placed her mug in the sink, rested her backpack on Anna's chair, and took her seat. She sighed, leaned back, and crossed her legs.

"Okay, go."

"I got *three-bombed*. Straight three-bombed." I thrust my evaluation sheet into her unamused face. "On a scale of dingus to surgeon, I earned straight threes across the board, AKA *average*. Mediocre, middle-of-the-road, unremarkable..."

"I'm familiar with the term."

"And *worse*—I got canned comments."

"What do you mean canned?"

"*Ugh! Canned!* Like Campbell's freaking chicken soup. Mass-produced. Copied and pasted from some bank of suggested feedback. Look!" I took the paper out of Dani's hands and read aloud in a mocking tone, "Appropriate fund of knowledge for level of training. Able to form clinical questions. Expected performance. Meets obligations."

"Ah, yes…Campbell's comments…" She mocked me.

"Do you not see why this is devastating?"

"Sam." She took a deep, slow breath and closed her eyes like she was gathering patience from the depths of her soul. "It's your first two weeks of clinical rotations. Ever. Did you expect to go in there and act at the level of an intern, having never even worked on a clinical team before?"

I did… That's exactly what I expected. I scowled at her.

She continued, "You're a competent person. Give yourself some time to work your way up the scale."

Bringing my aggravation down to a simmer, I replied curtly, "I guess you're right."

Nodding, she took the paper out of my hand, folded it up, and tucked it back in the torn envelope.

"So where's this node?"

"*Ugh*! The node! Good *grief*, look at this…"

She went through a thorough history-taking, which I appreciated, as she palpated the nodule in my neck.

"Sam…I'm not a doctor…" She joked, then cringed and continued gently, "But I really think that it's fine. Remember when you thought you had brain tumor because your pupils *maybe* looked different sizes? Then you signed up to be a participant in that MRI study just to make sure?"

"Yes."

"Then you thought you had hypothyroidism because you were gaining weight and were cold all the time and felt like you had 'mental slowing?'"

"Yep."

"And then you thought you had nephrotic syndrome when your pee looked like it had bubbles in it?"

"What's your point?" I asked dryly.

She tilted her head at me with her "shut-up-and-get-it-together" smirk, then got up and left the kitchen. As she climbed the stairs toward her bedroom, she remarked over her shoulder, "Stop creating problems that you don't have. Like lymphoma and incompetence."

"So you *did* consider lymphoma on your differential?"

She firmly closed her door behind her.

I packed up my books from the kitchen table and retired to my own bedroom. Lying on my bed in my work clothes, I dejectedly rubbed my node. It felt smaller than I remembered it. *She's right. I'm overreacting. I need to relax. How am I going to be a surgeon if I can't focus? Focus, Sam.*

Cracking open my laptop with every intention of studying, I propped myself up with pillows and got comfortable. Rookie mistake. I basically dug my own grave. I fell asleep right there, reading about how tuberculosis can cause enlarged lymph nodes.

CHAPTER 13

MENTAL STATUS CHANGES

ANNA

    Some people thrived on night shift. I was simply not one of those people.

    Those people reminded me of vampires, sitting around the workroom in the dark, faces glowing in the light of their computer screens. They were the equivalent of bloodthirsty savages—waiting for midnight bedlam, any form of excitement to keep them active until the sun rose and they slunk back to their coffins.

    Perhaps that's a bit harsh.

    I couldn't relate, operating with constant brain fog and repeatedly counting down the minutes until morning signout. The vampires loved it for a reason, though. Night shifts had been incredibly hectic lately with obstetric emergencies and back-to-back-to-back deliveries. Thankfully, it was my last night shift, and I would have the entire weekend off before returning to a more human schedule on the gynecologic surgery team.

As I walked into the evening sign-out, it became clear that my last night shift would be the grand finale. Every patient room was filled. Our unit was planning to go on diversion, meaning that we simply couldn't accept any more laboring mothers at our hospital. We would still see any potential emergencies, obviously, but if the baby could wait, then the baby would have to wait.

A skeleton crew—Bitchy-Rachel, a junior resident, an intern, and I—would be staffing the floor. The attending, who usually only appeared when moms began pushing, announced that we'd need all hands on deck.

I scribbled notes on my patient list. *Let's do this.*

I had become significantly more comfortable with my role over the two weeks on the labor and delivery service. Even on the slow days, I'd seen multiple deliveries. I figured out the rhythm and routine. Feeling confident, I immediately volunteered to see the patient in triage sent up from the emergency department. Keeping the initial encounter brief but comprehensive, I anticipated that—from my medical student perspective—the patient would be safe to discharge home.

Waiting to present the information I'd gathered to an actual doctor, I stood at my hallway computer and typed up my assessment. My notes were practiced and polished. I followed the specific format, a satisfying algorithm: ask all the questions, check all the boxes. I felt helpful by writing notes, like I was doing something right.

Bitchy-Rachel turned the corner and power-walked toward me. "I'm going to discharge that triage patient so that we can keep things moving."

"I saw her and already typed up the note," I reported with some pride.

"I went in right after you to see for myself. You know that I write all my own notes. It's just easier that way. You can delete yours."

Clearly, I didn't know that. Has she been looking at my notes this week at all? How is she supposed to evaluate me if she didn't read them? What am I even good for?

"Oh…okay…well…what can I do to be the most helpful then?"

She grumbled as she banged on the keyboard. "I guess just follow along with me for now."

My last night shift, and I'm stuck being Bitchy-Rachel's shadow. Just my luck. It's fine…I'll show her that I know some things.

As we ventured into the first delivery room, I stepped right into the routine I had mastered: set up the delivery cart, hand out blue gowns, pull sterile gloves. I had memorized the sizes of everyone on the team at that point. When I went to put on my own gown, after ensuring everyone else was ready to go, Bitchy-Rachel stopped me.

"That won't be necessary. I've got it under control, and we need to get on to the next one, so just stand behind me."

Stand behind you? I've been in the room for at least twenty deliveries at this point. I've gowned up for every single one of them. I've delivered the placenta myself during most of them! Sometimes I even guided the baby out with the help of someone else on the team. I am not *useless. Why wouldn't you want another set of hands to line up instruments, clamp the cord, clean up as you work? Come on! You could use me, and you know it.*

"Okay."

She handled the delivery like a true professional. Everything—the reassuring way she coached the mom along, the confidence in her technique, the efficient cleanup—was incredible. *Maybe she didn't need me after all.*

I followed her like a duckling into and out of delivery rooms. I stood behind her in awe each time. In the middle of our fourth—yes, *fourth*—delivery, an announcement boomed overhead.

"Any available resident to room nine. Any available resident to room nine."

Bitchy-Rachel, touching the crown of the baby's head as it poked out from his mom, mumbled under her breath and huffed, "Can you go see what that's about?"

Me? They said "any available resident..."

The intern was in room two and had been for a while at that point. The junior resident was in the OR with the attending, delivering twins. I jogged to room nine.

Thankfully, I'd met all the patients earlier. I learned to introduce myself to each of them at the beginning of my shift. Inevitably, I'd get called into a room during a delivery, and it was painfully awkward to introduce yourself to a woman with a little human already coming out of her cervix.

Like the mom in room nine at that moment.

Two nurses—the oldest and youngest on the floor—were already gowned up. Mom was red in the face, screaming, while Dad was white in the face, silent. The room smelled like childbirth, thick with the sweaty metal aroma of blood plus other things I tried very hard to ignore as I got closer.

The older nurse, Jan, stood at the delivery cart between Mom's legs and clapped together her gloved hands.

"Gown up, sweetheart. This baby isn't going to wait."

She knows I'm the medical student, right? We've been in multiple deliveries together. She was the one who taught me how to collect cord blood. She definitely knows that I'm just a medical student. Right?

The new nurse, Jess, was at Mom's bedside to the right, holding her hand and coaching her breathing. She was about my age and still in training, much like myself. She offered me an expression of pity.

"The on-call attending has already been paged and is on his way."

Okay...well...they called for backup. This should be fine, then?

As I joined Jan, I held up my ID badge and tapped the capitalized text in red at the bottom: MEDICAL STUDENT.

"I know," she said as she handed me a gown and pointed at the baby's full head of black hair peeking out of Mom's vagina.

Oh no, she wasn't kidding...

I rapidly pulled on my gown and gloves and took in the rest of the scene. Baby's and Mom's vitals were perfectly stable. Contractions were regular and sufficient. Everything on the delivery cart was already prepped.

I guess I'm going to deliver this baby.

In my adult voice, I echoed the words I had heard in every other delivery.

"Alright, Mom, we're going to start pushing just like we've practiced before, okay? On three..."

Everything was going smoothly. Every ten seconds or so, Jan nodded at me for positive reinforcement. We had this under control. *Babies come out on their own all the time, anyway, right?*

After the fourth or fifth round of pushing, the on-call attending sauntered in. Of course, he and I had never met before. Dr. B had just returned from a few weeks of vacation. Meeting your supervisor for the first time while you're between your patient's legs might be even worse than meeting your patient for the first time down there.

He greeted the patient calmly as he read the monitor and surveyed the room.

What am I supposed to say? Hi Dr. B, I'm the medical student?

Jan, thankfully, caught him and whispered in his ear.

His eyes widened as they met mine, but he stayed cool as he stepped over to join me.

"Keep going," he instructed.

"Alright, Mom, I want you to give me a big push here, ready..."

That was all it took—one more push—for the baby's head to pop out entirely.

"Okay, Mom, relax for a second..."

"Check for a cord," Dr. B directed as my fingers were already in the process of doing so, swiping around the baby's neck.

"No cord," I whispered.

"Great, keep going."

I braced myself, "Alright, Mom, and again..."

After a few more pushes, I helped Baby Boy safely onto Mom's chest. He cried, Mom cried, Dad cried, and I could have cried, but I wasn't done yet. As Jan helped Dad cut the cord, I delivered the placenta. Dr. B quietly observed as I performed a final exam. The uterus was firm, and I detected only minimal bleeding from the cervix. I was relieved, for Mom and myself, to find no lacerations. When the baby had been cleaned and swaddled and returned to Mom and Dad, they thanked me. Mom squeezed my hand, and Dad was so happy that he hugged me.

That might have been the most rewarding thing I've ever done.

We cleaned up quickly to give the family some time to enjoy the precious moment. On our way out of the room, Dr. B patted me on the back. "How many deliveries have you done now?"

I caught Jan's eye, and she smiled.

"One," I admitted sheepishly.

Dr. B chuckled. "Well done."

At morning sign-out, the team tiredly clapped for ourselves when the attendings congratulated us on making it through a night from hell: ten deliveries, all very successful. *What a night it was.* I collected my belongings from the resident room and prepared to say goodbye to everyone. I would be working with different residents during the surgery portion of the Ob-Gyn rotation.

I awkwardly stood in the doorway like a pack mule with my overly stuffed backpack, coat draped over my arm, lunchbox in one hand, coffee mug in the other, and a dumb smile on my face. "Thanks so much for everything the past couple of weeks, you guys."

The intern and junior resident spun around in their chairs.

"Heard you did awesome last night!" The intern smiled with enthusiasm.

The junior added kindly, "You've been super helpful. Let us know if you need anything or if you decide you're interested in OB!"

Ringgg! Bitchy-Rachel snatched up the phone, not bothering to take a moment to say goodbye.

I didn't take it personally; I'd never heard her say thank you to anyone.

Good riddance.

I called my parents as soon as I got home, eager to share my win. Beaming the entire time, I rambled through the story to the point of becoming short of breath. "I walked in, and the baby was already poking out... I just about died when the attending got there... I don't think I took a breath the whole time...You should have seen the parents. They were so happy." When I finished, the other line was silent.

"Hello?" I probed.

"That's so great, honey!" Mom sounded...off.

Dad still hadn't said anything at all.

"Is everything okay?"

The long pause that followed answered my question. Something was not right.

"We have to tell you something..." Dad began.

"...and we want you to know that everything *is* okay—right now," Mom continued, "But it's time that you know."

The phone felt slippery as my palms began to sweat.

"Know *what*?" I held my breath.

"Honey," Mom cleared her throat, then stated plainly, "I have endometrial cancer."

Heat rose from somewhere deep inside of me as I half-listened to them justify a series of secrets.

"We didn't want to ruin the holidays..."

Ruin the holidays? They've known since the holidays? It's June right now, for crying out loud. I was home for the holidays. I was home for eight weeks after *the holidays! They thought it would be better to* call *me when I was hundreds of miles away?*

"Your sister doesn't know yet either..."

Of course, she didn't know. She would have lost her mind. If I didn't know, she certainly didn't know.

"We also didn't want to throw you off during Step 1 studying. The biopsy had just happened..."

She's already had a biopsy? During my study block...I mean, they were right. I would have been thrown off. I don't know what I would have done. But didn't they recognize that I could have been helpful?

"Hey—" I interjected. "So, what now? A hysterectomy? Then we know the stage?"

"Well, it's stage three."

"How can they stage it without taking out the uterus? I thought it couldn't be officially staged until a hysterectomy."

Silence, again.

"They took it out back in January."

"What do you mean they took it out?"

Their deceit doused my smoldering rage like gasoline. *January. I was home in January.* My parents welcomed me back into the house for my dedicated study period. I worked for twelve hours a day then joined them for a home-cooked meal almost every night. *How could my mom have appointments and an outpatient surgery without me noticing? Was I that wrapped up in my work?*

The answer was yes. I was so focused on my exam that I barely batted an eye when Mom "wasn't feeling well."

She let out a long, exasperated breath, and redirected the conversation. "My next appointment is this afternoon."

A minute later, I was already shoving clothes into a backpack, calculating how long it would take to get home with traffic, what time I would have to be back for my shift on Monday, and how many times my parents had lied to me. I poured two coffees for the road. Although I hadn't slept, I was pretty sure my fury would keep me awake.

One foot hard-pressed the gas pedal; the other *tap-tap-tap-tapped*, restively and offbeat from the car radio. My mind wandered to being home over the holidays. I could not understand why my mom had insisted on visiting the jewelry counter with my sister and me that day we went shopping. She just about dragged us to the ring section. The gemstones lining the display case gleamed unlike anything I ever owned. Mom didn't have anything like that either, only her modest engagement ring. The price tags, despite flaunting *"Holiday Special!"* reminded me why.

"You can each pick one out."

She had to be joking; she usually was.

"Okay, Mom." I attempted to quash it.

"I'm serious. Pick one." Her hazel eyes offered an unfamiliar sincerity.

My sister and I exchanged confused glances, then retorted, back-and-forth:

"That's unnecessary."

"These are so expensive."

"Come on, Mom."

"You know you don't even have to get us…"

Bang!

She slammed her hand on the glass display case and begged, "Damn it, girls, will you just do this for me?"

"Ha! Do this for *you*?" my sister sassed, eyebrows raised.

Mom chuckled and countered, almost earnestly, "Yeah, that way when I'm dead you can wear them to my funeral."

"*Mom!*" We disapproved in unison.

Her favorite ring in the entire display held a sapphire, hugged by tiny diamonds. It felt foreign on my finger the first few days, but by the time I returned to school, my hand felt naked without it. I realized now why she bought us the rings.

She thought she was dying.

The sun glared over the river as I sat in traffic on the bridge.

I glared back.

CHAPTER 14

UNSPECIFIED EARLY COMPLICATION OF TRAUMA

SAM

Here we are. New rotation. Two weeks down, one hundred and six to go. Where did the last couple weeks go, exactly? Oh, I know—down the shitter, with my grades and my future. Alright, so neurosurgery wasn't my forte, but maybe trauma surgery will surprise me.

Our new intern, Alex, showed Other Sam and me around the trauma unit. It was bustling with activity on a Monday morning. Alex was a tiny human, maybe pushing five feet, with a jaunty walk and an upbeat attitude. I could feel my double chin form when I looked down at her to make eye contact, so I mostly stared at the top of her head.

She spoke like a tour guide for children at a theme park. "Okay, kids. When a trauma comes in, grab blankets from the warmer over here. Have trauma shears ready to cut clothes. You'll find some in each bay if you don't have your own. Make sure you plug in the ultrasound machine, and turn it on if you anticipate that we'll need it."

While I was thrilled to be done with neurosurgery, I was still trying to wrap my head around the fact that our surgical subspecialty rotations were only two weeks long. After a mere two weeks, how could a medical student decide whether they wanted to pursue that specialty for their entire career? What if you had a great couple of weeks because the team was amazing, and then you were stuck with that specialty forever when it wasn't your calling? Or, what if you had a shit team and shit cases and you didn't give the specialty the consideration it deserved, and then you *missed* your calling? You can't just switcheroo between specialties after you commit.

When we settled into our new workroom—one with a large conference table in the center and a single computer in the corner being used by the chief resident—Intern Alex teed up the standard question: "Any idea of what specialty you might choose?"

I recited the same line that I used during the last rotation, the one that I assumed I would use for many months while still figuring it out: "I think I'm interested in surgery, but not sure yet. I'm just trying to keep an open mind as I go through rotations."

Other Sam chimed in, "I'm really interested in trauma, actually! I shadowed a trauma surgeon in my hometown over the summer."

Oh. My. Word. Is this guy serious? Has he changed his mind since last week when he was "really interested" in neurosurgery?

The chief resident, Jeff, chuckled. "Honestly, if there's anything that strikes your interest besides surgery, then do that." Intern Alex nodded solemnly in agreement.

All the surgical interns seemed like they were run into the ground. Why would anyone want that life? Med school is bad enough, but it looks like it's going to get worse in residency before it gets better. I've wanted to be a surgeon my whole life, but I imagined jumping straight to the attending part. I skipped right over school and residency in my mind. Idiot.

"For now, just hang out here until traumas come in. Tomorrow morning, you guys can round on the patients that we admit today." Chief Jeff and Intern Alex dipped out of the room, leaving Other Sam and me at the conference table.

Sweet, maybe I can get some studying done on this rotation after all...

As I opened my laptop, Other Sam kicked up his feet onto the chair next to him and rested his hands behind his head. "How's it going, man? You have a chill weekend?"

Man? Like we're buds now? And a chill weekend? Do I look chill to you?

I ruffled my hair, a mess of a mop. "Yeah, it was fine."

"We probably could use this time to study, but I just don't feel like it, you know? Knowing how to run through a primary survey should be enough to get us through our first day, I would think."

He's joking. He has to be... I skimmed some reading on the primary survey, but we wouldn't be the ones performing it, right? I thought we were just supposed to be towel-grabbers and clothes-clippers. "Ha...yeah, we'll see. I definitely need to get through some more of these practice questions."

"They're not that bad, dude. You'll crush them on the first pass."

As my computer loaded, I made sure my screen was tilted so that he couldn't see the "40% Correct" at the top of my last question block. When Chief Jeff crept back into the room at that moment, I awkwardly slammed my computer closed as if I were looking at something more inappropriate than my own inadequacy.

"Here," he threw a mess of supplies onto the table. "You guys can practice suturing during any downtime if you want."

Although I got three-bombed last week and could not perform a primary survey to save someone's life (literally), I did know how to sew up a laceration. Moms gave me my first suture practice kit in high school. It was pretty similar to the one I plucked from the supply pile dumped by Chief Jeff. The silicone pad, a low fidelity human skin model with precut wounds of various shapes and depths, felt familiar in my hands. Warming up, I threw a few simple interrupted stitches, then jumped right to practicing my vertical and horizontal mattress techniques.

Other Sam seemed to know what he was doing, sitting across from me in silence as he focused on a running stitch, but I undoubtedly had more reps under my belt. After a half-hour or so, the residents popped back in to check on us. Glancing over my shoulder, Alex did a double take at my suture pad.

"Sam, those are beautiful!"

"Thank you!"

My face promptly turned hemangioma red. Someone noticed me, and better yet, noticed that I knew how to do something.

Chief Jeff walked over to see what the fuss was about. "Nice! You know what, why don't you get some real practice? A patient that came in earlier this morning still needs a couple of small lacerations closed. She's in the corner bay. Ask the nurses for the lidocaine."

Intern Alex handed me three packs of sutures from her pocket as I stood up. Other Sam didn't look up from his work as I left the room and headed toward the nurses' station as if on a mission. *Maybe things will turn around for me... Maybe neurosurgery just wasn't the right fit, and trauma will be my time to shine.*

The patient in the corner bay was a sweet elderly woman recovering from a motor vehicle crash. She was resting her eyes, one of them underlined by a solid purple shiner. I gently knocked and introduced myself as the medical student, there to close her last few cuts from the accident.

"Oh, sure!" She waved me closer. "What grade are you in?"

The sincerity in her voice drove the knife in deeper. *What grade am I in? I'm in the nineteenth grade, ma'am.*

"I'm a third-year medical student."

"Oh, good for you! How many years left to go?"

"Well, two more years of medical school, then I have residency after that."

"And how long is residency, dear?"

"That will depend on which specialty I choose…"

"How exciting!" She beamed like she was actually proud of me. "What are you thinking?"

"I'm not sure yet." My voice carried false optimism. "Maybe surgery."

"Oh, you're going to be so good. I can tell. You have a sweet face."

"Thank you, ma'am."

Eff me. "*I have a sweet face.*" *I'm still going to look like an oversized middle schooler as an attending. The last time I checked, having a sweet face doesn't get medical students into surgical residencies.*

With cautious confidence, I carefully set up my work area. Next, I irrigated her wounds and numbed the areas with the correct amount of lidocaine, talking her through it every step of the way.

She stayed perfectly still, wincing only when I injected the analgesic around the cut on her head, right at her hairline. Her hair was dyed dark brown but showed some gray at the roots, and her skin was healthy and taut for her age. I wondered whether she had gotten Botox injections previously; I probably had more forehead wrinkles than her.

After waiting a moment for the medicine to kick in, I carefully stitched up the three lacerations and admired my work. The sutures were tidy and uniform; I was impressed and gladly announced, "You're all set!"

"Thank you so much, dear!"

She rifled through her purse as I cleaned up, eventually pulling out a pocket mirror in which she reviewed my work.

"Oh, they look wonderful. Good luck to you in your career!"

Proudly, I returned to the resident room where Other Sam was fumbling with his suture pad and trying to close a Y-shaped lac with some degree of difficulty.

"How'd it go?" he asked.

"It was good! Sweet lady." I tried not to sound smug, but I was.

I returned to my lac pad, pulling all the sutures out to start again. About ten minutes had passed when Chief Jeff poked his head in.

"Hey, Sam…can you come here for a sec?"

"Yeah," I scrambled to meet him in the hallway, "What's up?"

"What did you close those lacs with?"

"Um…"

Whatever I was handed…I didn't even think to check.

"I wouldn't have used the suture material you chose…"

He didn't look angry, just annoyed. I wanted to crumble into a pile of dust on the floor.

"Take out the forehead sutures and do it again with this instead. Thankfully it's right on her hairline. Next time just be sure to confirm what you're using with a resident."

But the intern handed me those sutures! Ugh. *This is bad. On top of being humiliated in front of my new chief, I need to go back in and tell this woman that I messed up.* I thought about banging my head against the door instead of simply knocking.

"Hi, ma'am."

"Hello, again!" she chimed cheerfully.

"Yes, ha...hello, again, um, I just spoke with my senior about the cut on your head. I know I closed it already, but we think it might heal even better if we stitched it using a different material instead. I'm sorry..."

"So you're going to take these out?"

"Yes..."

"Oh, shoot... Do you have to numb me again?"

"Yes..." I answered with uncertainty.

"Darn." She paused, tapping her fingers against her leg. "Do you really have to change it? Will it scar worse if you take these out and put new ones in?"

"Um...the doctor prefers that we close it using a different technique instead. It will heal better that way."

She winced. "I just really don't want to have to be stuck with a needle again... Can you ask him?"

"Ask him...?" I cringed.

"If we can just leave it?"

"Um...sure, let me see if I can find him. I'll be back."

Of course, he was nowhere to be found. I paced back and forth outside the resident room, just out of eyesight so that Other Sam wouldn't see me panicking. The nurses started watching me with suspicion, so I finally texted Chief Jeff.

> "Patient with head lac is asking if needs to be redone, doesn't want to be restuck with needle if she doesn't have to..."

> "Ok."

Okay, what? This is an SOS text, Chief! Mayday...dingus in distress. I need you to tell me what to do!

> "So should I redo it?"

> "Yes. Tell her we recommend."

As if I hadn't already... This'll be good.
I barely knocked as I plowed into the room for the third time.

"Hello, again."

She didn't look as enthused to see me and looked even less enthused as I stumbled over my own words, attempting to explain why we needed to take out her perfect yet incorrect forehead sutures.

"That's fine." She paused. "But I'm sorry dear...can someone else do it?"

"Of course!" My voice cracked. "Not a problem."

Tears were welling in my eyes as I walked out of the room. *Get it under control, Sam. Grow up.* I felt like I hadn't slept in days. *It's too early in a medical career to feel like this. Maybe I should have stayed on the waitlist where I belonged.*

I texted Chief Jeff again.

> "Patient would prefer if someone else changed out her sutures"

"*Then tell her it's fine.*"

"*Alright, do you want to do it or should I find Alex?*"

"*I mean tell the patient that it's fine, and we don't have to redo it.*"

Is this real life? I have to go back in there again *and tell her I was wrong* again? Absolutely reeling, I wiped my eyes on the sleeve of my white coat. I started to type out a rebuttal.

"*Maybe we can just—*"

I backspaced.

"*Maybe we can talk with—*"

I backspaced again.

"*I will talk with the patient again but maybe—*"

I cleared the text box and messaged back: "*Ok.*"

CHAPTER 15

IRRITABILITY

DANI

"*Doctah Dani!*"

I jumped half a mile in the air, having been focused on reviewing my Monday to-do list while standing in the hallway. Mr. Fruit Cup shuffled toward me with a walker. He wore a hospital gown with fresh breakfast stains, ratty sneakers, and a Cheshire Cat smile on his face. His physical therapist was also beaming, laughing, even. She trailed him closely with an arm outstretched behind, herding him down the hall. He waved to everyone he passed. "Guh-day! Guh-mornin'!"

He stopped when he reached me. "Doctah Dani, she said you can take me on walks!"

"That's great! I'm so happy to see you out of bed!"

"What time you comin'? You promised."

My schedule had become a clusterfuck. I pushed myself to pick up more patients and was trying to take more responsibility for each one. *And I did promise... I usually had an afternoon lull when I would attempt to catch up on reading and notes, but I could swing fifteen minutes to lap around the floor. I could probably use the exercise, too...*

"I can't give you an exact time, but after lunch for sure."

Later, barreling out of the noon education session, I realized I still had not had lunch, but wanted to catch Mr. Fruit Cup before I got sucked into doing something else. He was waiting for me, his arms crossed tightly over his chest.

"Mr. Fruit Cup! How's your afternoon?"

"Not good." He huffed.

"What's going on?"

He slipped the pulse ox off his finger, swung his skinny legs over one side of his bed, gripped his walker, and pulled himself up. He slowly and shakily started toward the door, motioning for me to join. The back of his gown was untied, his bottom completely exposed.

"Mr. Fruit Cup, let me close your…" I quickly grabbed the strings and tied a knot, allowing him some decency.

"I don't give a rat's ass," he snarled.

"Just let me…" I appealed cautiously as I finished securing the top and bottom. "What's going on?"

"They wanna send me to a facility."

He started shuffling down the hallway faster than I thought possible, thrusting his upper body forward with the walker and dragging his lower body to catch up. In finally allowing physical therapy to evaluate him, Mr. Fruit Cup had been given official discharge recommendations—to go to a subacute rehab facility.

"How do you feel about that?"

"Doctah Dani," he shook his head solemnly but maintained his hurried pace, "you gotta know something about me. I'm a dyin' man. A slowly dyin' man. I know we all slowly dyin', but some things make it go just a lil faster. Some things you choose. Like heroin. Other things you don't, like your wife dyin'."

We turned the corner around the nurses' station to venture down the longer hallway.

"You know, I shoulda been a youth counselor. I had a chance at a job when I got outta prison and was doin' good. I coulda helped the others, the younger guys. I chose to do other stuff instead. Silly stuff. I was still young. I think I coulda really helped them boys. I guess I coulda been a preacher too. That or a youth counselor."

Where is he going with this?

"Everyone keeps sayin' I need to go to a facility to get stronger. Get stable. Well, I ain't gonna get stronger. I know if I go to a facility, I'm gon' die there. They won't let me leave because I won't get stronger, and I'll die there. And I wanna die at home. I just want to die in my home, in my bed, where she died. So, when I close my eyes, I can wake up next to her."

He stopped abruptly, winded. Between breaths, he uttered, "Please let me die at home, Doctah Dani. You gotta tell 'em." A single tear rolled down his cheek, and he tucked his chin to his shoulder to wipe it away.

I knew there was no way he'd be discharged home. Physical therapy wasn't going to change their recommendation, and his case manager would already be looking for a bed for him. His medical reasons for hospitalization had improved. He was lucky they even deemed him appropriate for subacute rehab versus acute, where he would be expected to participate in even more significant therapy.

"I don't know—"

"Just fuckin' forget it," he snapped. "You're just like the rest of 'em."

His words stung, and I was stunned, frankly. *This wasn't my fault. How can he flip a switch so quickly, after all we've been through? He knows me... He knows that I care. Right?*

Mr. Fruit Cup turned away, slothfully and with contempt, and started back toward his room.

I didn't say anything but stayed two steps behind him until he made it safely back into bed.

Before sign-out at the end of the day, I updated the team about Mr. Fruit Cup's subacute rehab recommendation. Despite everything, he was really Jay's patient, not mine; in these situations, the resident made all the real decisions, signing all the notes and orders. They had the MD or DO at the end of their name, after all.

I also wanted to warn Jay about the reaction I received. "He's not really happy about it…"

"Well, tough shit. He doesn't have another option. Even if he tried to leave against medical advice and dragged himself all the way out of the hospital and into a cab, he'd be back in a week for a fall and a head bleed. Try telling him *that*."

"Yeah…I just wanted to let you know."

"Thanks. Good job today. Keep it up. You should get out of here, and we'll see you tomorrow."

"Thanks. You guys have a good night."

Tempted to try to make amends, I looked down the hall at Mr. Fruit Cup's open door as I left the unit. But I kept walking. *Is he right, that we're all slowly dying?* My mind floated back to preclinical lectures, to shortening telomeres and aging cells. It may not be heroin or the death of a loved one, but I wondered if medical school made the process go just a little bit faster.

* * *

Sam was making a mess all over the kitchen when I got home. There were breadcrumbs scattered across the counter and clinging to his shirt, dirty knives crisscrossed on the table, and open jars with one lid on the stove top and another on the floor. *How is it possible to create such chaos when making a peanut butter and jelly sandwich?*

"Where is Anna?" he demanded when I walked in the door.

"Hi, I missed you, too."

"I'm just saying, she fell off the face of the Earth, and I've noticed."

"She ended up driving home this weekend."

Anna sent me a cryptic message saying that a family thing came up and that she would be back by Monday. It wasn't unusual for her to be mysterious about personal goings-on, but I was a little surprised that she didn't say anything more. Getting up and driving states away in the middle of a rotation seemed a bit rash for her.

"Like home, home?" Sam remained incredulous.

"Yes, to Massachusetts."

"*What?*" He yelled and exposed the chewed sandwich in his mouth.

"Yep."

"In the middle of Ob-Gyn?"

"Yes." I retrieved my leftover chili from the fridge.

"Spontaneously."

"Yes." Cracking the Tupperware lid, I balked at the five-day-old, stewed pepper smell.

"Did someone die?"

"I'm not entirely sure what's going on, but it would have to be something significant for her to up and leave like that."

"Why didn't she tell us? How did I not know this?"

"We all have shit to deal with, and she'll talk about it when she's ready."

Anna tended to let her emotions brew until they boiled over. Even if I probed, I often was unsuccessful in soliciting her true feelings.

"So I shouldn't text her about it right now?"

"She'll talk about it when she's ready," I reiterated, annoyed. I punched a minute and a half on the microwave, which loudly started whirring while Sam pestered me.

"Feel my node again."

"It feels the same."

"You didn't even feel it." He pulled my fingers back to his neck.

"Ew, put some lotion on your sandpaper knuckles."

"Do you feel it?"

"Yes! I feel it!" I snapped, raising my voice.

"Whoa, tiger…"

"I'm sorry…today was just frustrating."

Sam became wide-eyed, anticipating that I was about to share feelings, showing that he was already uncomfortable.

"Do you want to talk about it, bud?"

"No."

"Can I talk about something?"

I rolled my eyes. "Of course, Sam."

"You know, this isn't fair, that you and Anna get to stay on the same rotation. Like I have to move on to a whole new surgical subspecialty while you're still on internal medicine and she's just on a different Ob-Gyn team."

"What, like it's comfortable?" My voice still carried notes of anger. I tried to adjust. "We're going to have the same flip-flopping when we switch blocks."

He nodded at the floor blankly.

"Are you good, Sam? You seem just a little more anxious than normal."

"This is my new baseline."

"We're all finding our new baselines, I guess."

We consumed the rest of our meals in silence while our exhaustion consumed us.

CHAPTER 16

FATIGUE

ANNA

Mom's appointment was a blur. The oncologist, a younger woman with horn-rimmed glasses and dimples, patiently answered my twenty questions. My parents made sure to tell her upfront that I was a medical student, which made me want to crawl under a rock. *Hi, real doctor, our daughter is a wannabe who knows some things.* I suppose she talked to me knowing that my medical literacy was a bit more significant than the average person, but I was embarrassed by my status, nonetheless.

I wondered what Mom's progress notes said. *A fifty-eight-year-old woman with no significant past medical history...* My parents kept it cool throughout the entire appointment, whereas I was on the verge of tears the whole time. At some point, I realized their composure drew from the fact that it wasn't their first rodeo. They had been going to appointments for months and months without me.

After, my thirty-six hours at home played back in a continuous loop in my head until a truck driver laid on the horn behind me. I stared blankly at the green light for a second, then resumed my commute into work. Weekend traffic put me home close to three in the morning. I barely slept in anticipation of the first surgery clinic shift on my Ob-Gyn rotation—precisely what I needed with endometrial cancer at the forefront of my mind.

What am I going to tell Sam and Dani?

Mom was starting her treatment at the end of the week. I would be driving home again, leaving directly from my Friday shift. I'd be there mainly for moral support. *What else is there for me to do for her? A whole lot of nothing.*

As I pulled into the employee garage, C called me. *It's seven in the morning... She's not usually awake yet. Did something happen to Mom?*

"Hello?" I answered with panic in my voice.

Only muffled sniffling came through from the other line. "C?"

She attempted to get out a greeting, then just started outright bawling.

"C, is everything okay?"

"An—*snffff*—Anna," C breathed in deeply, "I'm a mess."

"I see that..." I said cautiously as I noted the time on the car radio clock. Being only ten minutes early was cutting it a little close; I had no idea where the clinic was in the hospital. But I couldn't just hang up on C.

She was still reeling from the announcement. Before Mom's afternoon appointment on Saturday, we sat down as a family and told her everything. Tears had streamed down her face as she shook her head at me, like all of it was my fault.

"You knew? You fucking knew already? And no one told me? What kind of family keeps a fucking secret like that?"

We hid it to protect you. Just like they hid it to protect me at first, I guess.

"Language, Cynthia. Please." Dad pleaded, with guilt in his voice.

"But you're okay, r-right?" She shakily turned to Mom. "Like, you're getting treated, and you're going to be okay?"

"We hope so, honey."

"Anna, I just —*snffff*—k-keep thinking the worst and—*snfff*."

"C, I'm about to go into work, but listen—we have a plan. Mom is getting help. She's seeing some of the best cancer doctors in the world, and this treatment is the best option out there."

I shut off the car and reached for my white coat in the back seat. "I'll be back home at the end of the week, and I'll call you as soon as I get out later today. Everything's fine. Everything's going to be fine."

Her tone changed instantly as she snapped, "You always fucking say that, Anna, and it's clear that you don't even believe it yourself."

"I'll call you later."

Knowing that she would continue to meltdown when we got off the phone, I felt terrible hanging up. Yet, I was late to clinic. I couldn't remember the last time I was late for anything or the last time I was so exhausted that I didn't seem to care. *Other people were late to things all the time in real life, right? I could give an excuse, I suppose. Sorry I'm late, my mom has cancer, and my family is falling apart?*

When one of my new residents, Toria, greeted me, she didn't seem to notice the time, so I just kept my mouth shut.

In one breath, she rambled, "Okay, so on Mondays, we have clinic. The rest of the days, you'll be in the OR. You can see patients on your own. Just get a history to discuss with the attending. Today, it's Dr. Perez. She'll likely ask a few questions, and then we'll go back into the room together. You can go see the seven thirty appointment. They've already been roomed."

I glanced around the workroom for an available computer or even a chair on which to rest my things, but the residents were already basically sitting on top of each other.

"Oh, it's a little cramped in here…" Toria caught me looking around. "Just put your stuff in this corner and don't worry too much about reading up on the first patient. It's just a chemo follow-up, stage three endometrial cancer. Ask whatever questions you want, then just confirm what round it is and if she has any side effects."

My stomach sank into my pelvis.

I knew this was going to happen. An endometrial cancer patient was bound to show up to clinic today. It's gyn-onc clinic for crying out loud. I played this exact scenario out in my head during my drive back, and here we are. Ugh. Everything's fine…

Only one patient room had the door closed: the one tucked in the back corner of the clinic. I adjusted my white coat collar while peeking at the registration sheet in the plastic wall file on the door.

Ms. Costello, sixty-four years old. Only a few years older than Mom.

I exhaled deeply as I knocked. *This poor woman is here because she has cancer, and I'm going to ask her a million questions just for completeness of my presentation when she could just be seeing her doctor…who would simply confirm which round of chemo she's on and if she has any side effects.*

With fake cheeriness, I greeted the patient. "Hello, Ms. Costello. My name is Anna Cameron, and I'm the medical student working with your team."

"Nice to meet you." She spoke quietly and tersely and appeared older than sixty-four. Her hair was short, thin, and mostly gray except for occasional black streaks.

"How are things going for you?"

"Ha…well, they're going," she said somewhat brightly.

I bet that's exactly what Mom says in all her appointments. That would be just like her, to minimize the situation, to be nonchalant. Focus, Anna.

"How have you been feeling?" I pressed. "And which round of chemo is this?"

"Round three of Carbo-Taxol," she sighed. "Three more to go. You know, after the first couple rounds, I thought things would get better." She paused and wrung her hands. "Well, after surgery, I thought things would get better. But this pain in my hands and feet is horrible."

"I'm sorry to hear about the pain. When did that start?"

As she explained, I reviewed my mental notes—*Round three of carboplatin and paclitaxel combination therapy. She's had surgery. The surgery on its own was not curative. The cancer had already spread, so she needed chemo, which has a million side effects. One of those side effects is peripheral neuropathy.*

"Well, it started after the first round, but it's just gotten worse. And my hair is so thin." She ran her fingers through her curls.

I imagined what Mom might look like after chemo and radiation. *Will she lose her hair? Will she be able to keep her dark, beautiful braids? Will she cut her hair short preemptively?*

"Can you describe the pain for me?"

"Pins and needles, in every finger and every toe. Sometimes numbness, but usually just the pain. I took that gabapentin for a couple of weeks after the first round, but it made me feel just awful, like I was in a fog...and I'd rather be in pain."

Mom would lose her mind if she had to deal with brain fog. No one has a more active mind than she does—and if she isn't able to function at the same level she used to before treatment, I don't know how that will impact her mental health...

"And, um." *What next, Anna? Focus on the patient in front of you.* "Uh, okay, Ms. Costello, how long ago was the hysterectomy?"

"Almost six months now."

"Was it laparoscopic?"

"Yes. And they had to take my ovaries, too."

"No surgical complications?"

"No."

What else do I need to know... How did I let myself lose my train of thought? Where is my mental checklist?

I stalled. "Forgive me for asking so many questions. I just want to make sure I cover all my bases."

"I understand, dear."

"Have you, uh, had any other symptoms?"

I sound like an idiot. How could I be so unprepared?

"Um, occasionally, I feel a little more tired than usual, but that's all."

"Any nausea or vomiting?"

"Only right after the infusion."

Luckily, I remembered the rest of the potential side effects, which I'd just about burned into my brain over the weekend.

She shook her head as I ran through each item: "Abdominal pain, diarrhea, constipation, easy bleeding or bruising, joint pain, body aches, weakness?"

"Okay, I'm just going to do a quick physical exam; then I'll come back in with Dr. Perez."

"Sure thing, dear."

Okay...again, what do I know? A sixty-four-year-old female with stage three endometrial carcinoma status post uncomplicated total abdominal hysterectomy and bilateral salpingo-oophorectomy six months ago and carboplatin/paclitaxel treatment presents for follow up. Patient received three out of six rounds of chemo. She endorses progressively worsening peripheral neuropathy in bilateral upper and lower extremities for six weeks, which she describes as pins and needles in every finger and toe with occasional numbness. Additionally, she's had hair loss and fatigue. That sounds good to me...

Reciting that confidently to Dr. Perez seemed to earn me some points, but just as Toria warned, she hit me with a barrage of follow-up questions.

"What makes her cancer stage three?"

"Do you know how carboplatin works?"

"How about paclitaxel?"

"What labs should we be monitoring?"

And, finally, "What's the survival rate?"

"Well, um...it depends on whether it's localized, regional, or distant at the time of diagnosis," I began.

"Let's say it's regional, like Ms. Costello's."

And like Mom's...

"Somewhere around seventy percent."

She raised her eyebrows, surprised that I knew the answer.

"Excellent." She used my word.

Is it? Is that excellent? What if Mom gets worse? How can I help her if I'm here? Do I take a leave of absence? Would that totally throw off my path to residency?

When we went back in to see the patient as a group, Dr. Perez re-asked many of the same questions I had. Ms.

Costello looked at me each time she answered, as if to say, *I just told you this...* I apologized with my eyes.

Dr. Perez stood up at the end of her questioning. "Alright, well as I mentioned, your labs all look great, and things seem to be going okay. You have your next round in two weeks, and we'll touch base then. What other questions do you have?"

"No more questions, doctor."

That's it? That was the entire point of this appointment? There's nothing else we can do for her? We just wait?

A tear formed in the corner of my eye, balancing for a moment and wiggling before I wiped it away and excused myself to the bathroom. My exhaustion was lowering my threshold for emotional collapse. Sniffling in the hallway outside of the clinic, I walked past the one and only Bitchy-Rachel, presumably on her way to the cafeteria. It was too late to avoid making eye contact once I saw her, and embarrassment over my teary eyes and red cheeks instantly consumed me. Ultimately, it didn't really matter, because she immediately looked away, and we both just kept walking.

In the bathroom, I wiped off the makeup under my eyes and gave myself a mirror pep talk. *Get it together. What would Mom say? You need to power through. I will power through.*

And that's what I did—I made it through the rest of clinic—but couldn't bring myself to leave at the end of the day. When I was dismissed, I wandered to the hospital library and took out my computer to bury myself in work. After a couple hundred practice questions, my computer battery died abruptly. *Ugh.* My charger was in my weekend bag in the car. *How did I leave it there? I never used to be this disorganized.*

Pulling my phone out of my pocket, I realized that time had really gotten away from me. *Nine o'clock!* Multiple unread texts aggressively questioned my whereabouts, so I packed up hastily and made my way home.

Dani sat at the kitchen table with her study materials spread out, pretending like she wasn't there to wait up for me.

"Hey, stranger. How's it going?"

"Everything's fine."

She knew not to believe me. I texted her on Saturday to tell her that I was going home for a family thing and not to worry. Dani never pushed me. She knew that I would talk when I was ready. Our relationship had grown to be one of the more emotional friendships I'd ever had, but I could still count on one hand the number of times I had cried in front of Dani. She conveniently wasn't a crier either, though I witnessed some serious waterworks during her breakup our first year of medical school.

When the tears started rolling down my face, she handed me a tissue from a box she had hiding next to her.

"I don't really want to talk about it," I said.

"Then don't. Just remember you're not alone."

CHAPTER 17

HEADACHE

DANI

Someone was being murdered. I had no question in my mind when I heard the blood-curdling screams erupting from the kitchen. My first instinct was to grab the beat-up Louisville Slugger leaning in the corner of my bedroom—the one that used to live behind the bar next to the cash register—and barrel down the stairs. As I hit the bottom step, I gripped the duct-taped handle with both hands and loaded the bat over my right shoulder.

"*Oh my god. Make it stop. Oh my god!*"

"*Please, please, please, please!*"

Sam and Anna took turns shrieking from their perches, both of them balancing on kitchen chairs as a massive grasshopper jumped from the floor to the windowsill, to the tabletop, and back to the floor, in a perpetual cycle. The bug was simply enormous. Its buzzing was loud enough to hear over the screeching and squealing of my unreasonably terrified roommates.

Anna held herself in a tight hug and stood on her tiptoes. Sam was actively trying to push himself as far as possible into the corner where the wall met the ceiling, like a demon during an exorcism. His neck was bent to avoid grazing his head, and his hands scratched at the wallpaper.

"*Dani! Hit it with the bat!*"

"*Oh my god! Dani! Get it!*"

"You guys have got to be kidding," I said as I laid my weapon to rest on the tile floor. The shouting continued as I picked up an empty water glass from the drying rack by the sink and got on my knees under the table. The insect monstrosity paused but continued to flex its meaty hind legs. I stayed perfectly still, prepared for a face-off. Its antennae twitched, and I could see the reflection of the kitchen windowpanes in its cold black eyes.

"*What are you doing?*"

"*Are you out of your goddamn mind?*"

Sam accidentally kicked the table with one of his flailing lower limbs, prompting the insect to pounce. I surprised myself when I snatched it out of the air, cupping it into the glass with my bare hand.

"*What is happening?*"

"*Did you get it?*"

Scooting backward out from underneath the table, I made sure to keep a tight seal. As I stood up, I lifted my hefty prisoner above my head like a trophy.

"You are a *saint*, Dani." Anna climbed down from her roost.

Sam stayed put in his corner. "Um, and a psychopath… Did you touch it?"

"You're both giving me a migraine. Someone open the door."

Anna obliged while Sam challenged, "What if it comes back in?"

"Then I'll catch it again."

I walked down our front steps to the sidewalk and marched all the way to the other end of the block. A park at the corner lined by dense shrubbery would do. Shaking the glass upside-down over the bushes, I mumbled to the freed beast, "Sorry about them…"

The cowards were both calmly seated when I returned. I wondered if they had been talking about why Anna went home; she still hadn't said anything to me, but I knew she was hurting. She didn't have the usual bounce in her step or command over household activities. We got a late notice for our electric bill, which she always paid, and never past due. She hadn't meal prepped for the week either and didn't offer a firm suggestion when takeout was discussed.

As I climbed onto my chair, Sam said, "I still don't know about that whole catch and release situation."

"You should probably get used to it before you rotate through hospital medicine," I remarked sarcastically.

Anna snickered as Sam furrowed his eyebrows. "What do you mean?"

"Catch and release—isn't that what we do? Isn't that the *goal* even? To catch an ailing patient, treat them, and release them back into the wild? I feel like dispo conversations are the bane of my existence these days." I deepened my voice, imitating Jay. "When can we get them out of here? How can we make them safe for discharge?"

Anna laughed. "Yeah, I mean the goal is that they don't bounce back into the hospital, right?"

"Right," I emphasized. "That's why you need to walk them all the way to the corner."

How many times did Mr. Fruit Cup bounce back? Was it because his dispo wasn't appropriate? Could the medical team have done something better, or can it not be helped?

* * *

Mr. Fruit Cup and I turned down the long corridor on our afternoon walk.

"I'm glad we made up," he said as we shuffled past the nurses' station.

I chuckled. "You're just glad you're on a walk with me instead of your physical therapist."

"You know, that is partially true."

We both giggled as we waved to the PT down the hall. The day after the whole falling out with Mr. Fruit Cup—the subacute rehab debacle—I felt absolutely crushed. Assuming that he never wanted to speak to me again, I prepared myself to pick up a new patient and transfer Mr. Fruit Cup to somebody else on the team. However, when I arrived at work, Kate, his nurse for the day, came into the resident room with a yellow sticky note.

"Dani," she said as she offered me the paper, stuck to her pointer finger, "someone wants to see you."

In shaky handwriting, the note simply read, "Dr. Dani."

"Why did he write that?" I asked, not understanding the need for the hard copy request.

"It's been on his side table since dinner time. I think he just wanted everyone to know that he was still expecting to see you this morning...even after he got a little upset with you."

I cringed. "You know about that?"

"We just talked about it five minutes ago." She offered a weak smile. "He really would like to see you."

I stuck the note to the front of my planner and tucked it into my pocket. When I softly knocked on the open door to his room, he was sitting up waiting for me, just like he had on our first good day.

"Doctah Dani, I owe you ah' apology."
I shook my head. "No, no. You don't owe me anything."
"Yes, I do. You were just tryin' to do your job. I shoulda just let you explain to me."
"I feel like I owe *you* an apology. I should have tried to— "
"I didn't let you," he interrupted and shook his finger at me. "Don' you ever let a man silence you, Doctah Dani."
"Well, then," I sassed, "stop cutting me off in the middle of my apology and let me get through my physical exam, Mr. Fruit Cup."
He laughed, and I knew we were okay.
Days later, as we sauntered around the unit, I was again grateful that we had made up. At that point, Mr. Fruit Cup was a classic "dispo issue." He was ready to go to subacute rehab, but a bed wasn't available yet. All his acute medical problems had resolved, and he had been getting stronger. He should have been stepped down from the intermediate care unit to a general medicine floor. Lucky for both of us, the hospital was dealing with its own bed issue, so he was staying put.
"Do you remember what you asked me a couple of weeks ago?" He questioned.
"A couple of weeks ago! I ask you a lot of things…"
He had become so accustomed to my daily interrogations that before I could ask he once rattled off, "And no, I haven't had any fevers, chills, nausea, vomiting, shortness of breath, chest pain, diarrhea, constipation, or any other damn thing."
He began, "You asked me if I thought somebody could help me find myself, so I thought about it more."
"And?"
"Well, I realized that Margot helped me find myself all those years ago."

"Margot?"

"My wife! Come on, Doctah, keep up!" He quickened his pace and edged past me in jest, then slowed again after only a few steps.

"Okay, okay. So, Margot helped you find yourself?"

"Yes. When I was with her, I felt no pain."

"You were really lucky to find someone like that."

"Doctah Dani, you're gonna find someone like that, too."

I raised my eyebrows at him, taken aback that somehow the conversation had turned toward me.

"You gotta start giving away more of your pieces."

Somewhat afraid to ask, I ventured, "What pieces?"

"Hold on, and I'll tell ya—you didn't let me finish. Margot, she helped me find myself. She was the love o' my life. But when she died, I never let anybody else in because I knew I was never gonna have that type of love again." He stopped to catch his breath. "But there are lotsa types of love out there. Not just the kind I had with Margot. And you gotta think about it like this, Doctah Dani. Think about...if you carried your heart in your pocket."

He made a heart shape with his hands and shook it in the air.

"And whenever you wanted, you could reach into your pocket and take a little piece. You could hand little pieces to whoever you wanted. When Margot passed, I kept mine deep in my pocket—I shoved it down in there—and I didn't give anyone a single piece. I was too afraid that if I started givin' 'em away, I'd run outta pieces."

Mr. Fruit Cup grabbed his walker and resumed his march to his room.

"But...bein' here in the hospital, I remembered, well...I'm slowly dyin', right? So what the hell, I started givin' 'em away.

I gave one to you, and I gave some to the nurses, and I even gave a little bit to that PT."

He flung imaginary heart fragments in the air.

"And you know what, Doctah Dani. My pocket feels heavier!"

We walked in silent reflection until I helped tuck him back into his bed.

My pockets are full of medical reference guides; I'm not sure there's any room for heart pieces in there. I thought becoming a doctor would make my heart feel fuller—like I was doing something important. Instead, my relationship shattered under the stress of it all, my friendships from before med school disintegrated, and my hobbies became memories. Am I doing this wrong?

Mr. Fruit Cup's voice quieted as he offered his final thoughts: "And you know, Doctah Dani, I never really had heavy pockets in my life. This might be as good as it gets for now. Givin' away some of the pieces makes all the pain a little more bearable. And it reminds me that, someday, I'll be back with Margot, and I won't feel any pain at all."

I gently squeezed his hand. "Well, until then, keep giving out those pieces."

"Hmph," he smiled, "you better start giving out yours."

CHAPTER 18

SYNCOPE

SAM

Cheese and rice. I'm out of shape. I huffed and puffed up three flights of stairs, trailing Intern Alex. I followed her to the other side of the hospital—literally, the absolute farthest possible point from the trauma bays—to *watch* her change a patient's bandage. Not even to change it myself. While catching my breath, I snapped on plastic gloves, even though I knew that I wouldn't be touching anything. *Maybe* I'd hand her some tape.

Alex pulled back a glorified Band-Aid on the patient's arm to reveal the world's tiniest stab wound. It looked like he had been stabbed by a scalpel, less than half an inch wide. *We power-walked a 5K for this?* The laceration was neatly closed and healing well. Alex took out her phone to snap a photo for the patient's chart.

"Oh, shoot! Sam, I forgot to take a picture of the burn downstairs in bay one. Can you run back down there?"

Do I look like an Olympian to you?

"Sure thing. That's within my skill set."

She cackled. *I'm going to milk that joke for all it's worth.* Her reaction exceeded what the quip deserved, her laugh toeing the line of maniacal. To be fair, she probably hadn't slept in days either.

Retracing my steps at a much slower pace, I ventured back to the trauma bays. *At some point, I'll have a real skill set. Maybe.*

The patient in bay one was a middle-aged suburban dad on his day off. While attempting to burn a pile of brush in his backyard, he thought it wise to hold his arm directly over the fire while actively dousing it with gasoline. The result wasn't pretty, but he got lucky in the grand scheme of burns. His barbecued arm was entirely wrapped up; the wound was neatly dressed. At this point, he was fast asleep and resting comfortably, as he should have been after being completely snowed with pain medication.

"Hello, sir..." I awkwardly tapped on his shoulder. He continued snoring. Louder, I said to the sleeping man, "I just need to take a picture of your wound for your chart so we can track your healing..."

Okay. Open the secure media file app. Pull up patient's chart. Rest phone over here. Sanitize hands. Put on gloves.

"Sir, I'm just going to lift up your arm here..."

I hoisted the patient's deadweight limb with one hand and began unwrapping it with the other: tossing the loose end of the gauze over his arm, then pulling it under, around and around. If Pyro-Dad was capable of holding up his own damn arm, it would have been a much neater process. I could have used two hands and tidily rolled the gauze as I went, but I had to work around the fact that he was drugged out of his mind. His arm felt heavier with each second, so I got faster and messier as I went.

When I finally reached the end of the ten-foot bandage, I set the patient's arm down on the gauze pile. Carefully, I started peeling back the next layer—a pearly white, goopy Silvadene dressing—when a shriek ripped through the room.

"*Eeeeeeeek!*"

I jumped and knocked my phone off the bedside table as a nurse charged toward me.

"*What the hell do you think you're doing?*"

"I need to take a picture—"

"I just finished this freakin' dressing!"

"I'm sorry, we just need—"

"I left it undressed for an hour. *One hour.* You could have taken as many photos as you like during that hour, but *now* you choose to come back and take down my dressing that took me *forty-five minutes*, and I have *two more patients* that need my attention, and another trauma is on its way?"

"I was just doing what I was told. I'm sorry…"

"Christ, just take your picture and let me fix this before the ambulance gets here."

She started ripping open the wound cart drawers, gathering new supplies and muttering under her breath. I caught every few words: "god damn students," "touch my perfect dressing," and "constant annoyance." Stooping under the miraculously still-snoring patient's bed, I picked up my phone from the filthy hospital floor. Its screen was cracked right down the middle, despite the tempered glass protector.

I can't win.

After snapping a photo of the patient's horrible burn, I mumbled thanks to the sleeping man and gowned up for the next trauma that was about to arrive. Banshee nurse bumped me out of the way as EMS wheeled in the new patient.

My core started to feel hot, which I attributed to the warm blankets I held as the screaming new patient was moved from the gurney to the bed by the other eight people in the room.

What the hell am I doing here? What did I think medical school was going to be like? When I was a kid, and the idea of being a surgeon was planted into my tiny impressionable brain, what did I think? Christ, I can't breathe.

I adjusted the mask over my face, pulling it off my mouth slightly, without improvement.

How about in college, when I was struggling through organic chemistry and working in a lab and juggling ten other extracurriculars, what did I think? That it was going to get better?

My heart was pounding in my chest; I heard the rapid *thump-thump-thump* over the chaos of the trauma bay. Someone ripped the blankets out of my hands. I was paralyzed. *Am I having a heart attack?*

As I struggled to inhale, beads of sweat popped up on my forehead, and the room became lighter, as if all color was being washed out. Activity continued around me like a dream—the attending calling out orders, the resident opening a kit to start a chest tube, a nurse getting a second IV—and I was floating, suffocating, watching it all.

I need to get out. I need to get out of here. I started pulling at my gown, but it was like my gloved fingers couldn't grip the plastic. *What is happening? Am I—*

Banshee nurse screamed before I hit the floor.

* * *

That little stunt landed me in therapy, as if I weren't embarrassed enough already. The brown leather squeaked if I moved even half a millimeter, so I sat statue-still on the office couch and took shallow breaths. The tiny room smelled like a thousand candles had been burning in it, so I wasn't sure how deeply I could inhale anyway. I suppose it could have been relaxing—some natural light seeping in through the dusty blinds, warm-colored furniture with throw pillows, the walls adorned with drawings of giraffes—but how was I supposed to relax during an initial patient visit when *I* was the patient?

The psychologist seemed nice enough: an ancient man with a thick white mustache and a beard to match. He wore miniature circular glasses, like John Lennon's teashades had shrunk in the dryer. His bowtie was definitely not a clip-on, and I hated the beige paisley pattern. Maybe I should have been honored to be psychoanalyzed by a relic of the Golden Age; he could have even been a classmate of Freud's, perhaps.

Dino-Shrink opened a desk drawer, and I half-expected him to pull out a tobacco pipe. Instead, he retrieved an empty manila folder and scribbled my name on the tab, barely legible.

"Why don't you tell me why you're here, Sam?" His voice was disappointing—toneless and adenoidal. I expected something silvery and distinguished.

I'm pretty sure my chief complaint is written on my intake form. I'm here because my friends made me come? Because I fell off the deep end? Because I have nothing better to do on a Friday afternoon? Should I say that?

"I had a panic attack."

"Have you experienced a panic attack before?"

"No."

"Have you dealt with anxiety in your life?"

Is this a rhetorical question?

"Yes."

"Why don't you tell me about medical school?"

"Do you have all day?"

He chortled. "Do you typically use humor to help you through difficult experiences?"

"Ha, like everyday life? It is one of the four mature defense mechanisms, you know."

"What brings you the most anxiety about medical school?"

"Oh, I don't know, that I've been bred to be a surgeon, and I might never reach my final form."

He held his pen in the air like he'd just dragged from a cigarette and gently nodded.

"Does surgery make you happy?"

Wow, he's going right for the jugular.

"How am I supposed to know what makes me happy?" I huffed. "I'm constantly trying to meet other people's expectations, figuring out which actions earn me the most points at the hospital, and struggling to stay sane at the same time."

"There's no formula, Sam. Why did you come to medical school in the first place?"

I felt my heart beating fast in my chest again.

"*I want to help people!* How's that? Everything about clinical medicine fascinates me—how we can cure infections with antibiotics, open up someone's belly to find and stop bleeding, look at an EKG strip and diagnose major heart conditions—it's amazing. Like, incredible. So, yeah, I like medicine, and I want to use it to fucking help people. Do I need a better answer than that?"

He remained still and let me ramble.

I spoke a mile a minute. "Are you looking for a more curated bullshit interview response like the one that got me into medical school in the first place? I just want to help people, but I haven't felt like I've helped a single person as a medical student. When does that change? When do I start to feel useful instead of like an idiot constantly?"

He twirled his pen and didn't flinch at all at my unraveling. He waited for me to continue, and when I didn't, he noted, "I think helping people and choosing medicine as your avenue to do so is a perfectly good reason. Why don't you feel like you've helped anyone as a medical student? What about your role reinforces that?"

"I'm rotating through surgery right now. The only time I'm useful in the OR is when I'm holding things open or I'm holding things closed, holding things up or holding them down. Outside of the OR, I can gather information to round on patients, but it takes my seniors the same amount of time to check my work as it would to just do it themselves. And I feel like I screw up constantly when really most things aren't my fault, but a fault of the system."

Dino-Shrink jotted something on his notepad. "It seems like a lot of your focus is on how you can help your *team*—your residents and attendings. But that's not why you're here, right? Did you come to medical school to help *them*?" He paused, looked at the giraffe in the wall, then back at me. "I'm sure everything you do contributes in some way to the workflow and to your education, but have you thought about how, as a medical student, you might be able to help your patients?"

I blinked at him in silence. *How did I let myself forget why I wanted to be here in the first place?*

He smirked as he watched me struggle. "Just something to think about."

CHAPTER 19

HYPERVENTILATION

ANNA

    I placed my mobile coffee order on the kitchen table as I waited for Sam to get his act together.

    "Fuck, fuck, fuck, fuck, fuck," he recited under his breath as he upturned couch cushions and sifted through stacks of papers on the counter.

    "You know if you always put your badge in the same place when you got home—"

    "*I know.*"

    "Did you check your—"

    "*Yes.*"

    "You don't even know what I was going to say."

    "I checked my backpack."

    "Did you check your car?"

    Sam stopped rifling through his backpack and cocked his head toward the ceiling, as if the answer was hidden in the popcorn texture.

    "It's in my car." He quietly admitted, nodding as he zipped his bag and grabbed his white coat from the hook on the wall. "What time is it?"

"6:37."

"Perfect, still plenty of time to cry in the parking lot."

Locking the door behind us, I wondered if anyone else joked the way that we did about going to work. Of course, we didn't cry in the parking lot each morning out of complete dread for the day to come. Well, at least I didn't. But some mornings I definitely sat in the driver's seat an extra few minutes for some deep breathing and a pep talk. Sam and I were both on clinic days, so we were going in later than usual to see our first patients. The crisp morning air still nipped at us on our walk to the parking garage.

"What a glorious day," I chattered.

Today wouldn't really warrant a cry for me because I'd be in the general gynecology clinic. No cancer today. I couldn't take another shift of gyn-onc. Then I maybe would have cried in the car.

Ten minutes after my first patient got roomed (and ten minutes after I should have been ready to see her) I restarted my computer on wheels for the second time. As if my lack of experience didn't hinder my efficiency enough, I had never logged into a hospital computer without issues—not once. If I had been able to pull up my patient's chart, I would have finished interviewing her already. Signing in would give me some idea of why the patient was coming into clinic—which was always preferable to going in blind—but I was getting anxious knowing that I could delay the whole clinic schedule for the rest of the day if I didn't get a move on. Abandoning ship, I asked the clerk for the age and chief complaint.

"Eighty-year-old female, genital lesion."

Damn it. If this is vulvar cancer, I quit. She's probably here for a gyn-onc referral. Why is cancer following me?

When watching medical videos online, I'd get targeted ads for American Cancer Society fundraisers and cancer support groups. Waiting for my coffee yesterday, I stood next to a nurse, mother, and her bald young daughter who was wearing a hospital bracelet and mask, apparently out for a walk from the pediatric oncology floor. She picked out a unicorn cookie, and the nurse bought her two.

I halfheartedly knocked on the exam room door as I opened it, offering a cheery "good morning!" I peeled back the curtain to find a very small, poised elderly woman with her legs crossed and hands folded over her knees. She wore a hospital gown that was much too large for her. Her floral print pants and light green sweater were neatly folded on the seat next to her. Transportation paperwork sat on the counter with "Shady Grove" stamped in large letters across the top. Shady Grove was the premiere retirement facility in the area. They didn't even brand it as a retirement community; it was billed as an "active adult community."

"Yes, good morning, dear," she squeaked, smiling.

"My name is Anna, I'm the medical student working with Dr. Grant today. I'm going to gather some information, and then Dr. Grant and I will come back in together to talk about a plan for you. Does that sound okay?"

"Of course, dear."

I took a seat on the rolling stool next to her so that we'd be at eye-level. Her gray eyes glinted underneath mild cataracts.

"Can you tell me about what brings you in today?"

"Well," she huffed and paused. "Some *bastard* gave me herpes."

My eyes widened then self-corrected. *Stop it...*

She continued, "And now I'm plotting his demise." She stated this matter-of-factly, then folded her arms and smirked.

This is rich. Finding composure, I nodded my head. "And, how, may I ask, are you doing that?"

I should have gotten right to the pertinent medical history questions; I was running late. *But the drama!* I was still composing myself and wanted to know if she was planning to kill this man. *I'd probably have to report that, right?*

"Oh, honey. I'm telling *everyone*. This man isn't going to be able to leave his room without being shamed. And he deserves it after what he did."

"What exactly did he do? Besides, you know—"

"He caused an outbreak!" She threw her hands into the air. "The whole community has it now! And I wouldn't be surprised if it made its way over to Pine Ridge and Water's Edge." She dramatically kicked out her legs as she name-dropped other retirement homes.

"I'm going to ruin his life," she chuckled.

I chuckled, too; I couldn't help myself. "Okay, so before you tell me the details of your master plan, can I ask you some medical questions?"

"Of course, dear." She recrossed her arms and legs.

A quick history-taking and physical exam confirmed her story. It was definitely herpes.

"Eh, what the hell," she shrugged her shoulders, "life goes on."

Walking back into the resident room to present the case to my senior resident, I continued to laugh. I shouldn't have, but this was a way better patient encounter than the vulvar cancer I was expecting. I knew the elderly population had increased incidence of sexually transmitted infections, but I imagined an isolated cesspool in central Florida or something.

I hid my smile while presenting the case to my new chief resident, and when I was finished, she *tsk-ed*, "Yeah, she's the third one this week."

"Well...Shady Grove does advertise itself as an active adult community..."

"*Ha!*" The resident shook her head, genuinely amused by me for once. "I'll go see her. You can start the note and then see room four."

My computer was still not logged on. I held the button down to restart it again, jotted down some notes on a piece of paper that I would eventually transcribe into the electronic medical record, and walked down the hall to room four.

Life goes on.

* * *

Later at home, my computer troubles continued. "Everything's fine," I repeated over and over in my head as I stared at the spinning wheel of torture in the middle of my screen. The last thing I needed was for my laptop to crash going into my last week of the block. Studying for Shelf meant we were cramming practice questions, daily flashcards, and trying to muck through the myriad of study resources to figure out what worked. By the time I determined what I liked best, it felt too late to effectively implement a study plan. *Maybe next block…*

Sam leaned way back in his chair with one of his legs extended straight out in front of him. His laptop was balanced half on the table and half on his lap, even though we had plenty of space for all of us to spread out. Dani leaned forward, her face only inches from her screen, baseball cap like a tent over her eyes, and elbows rested on the table. She had lit some candles, attempting to create an ambiance. I handed out cheese balls on little paper plates. Dani said she didn't want any and then snuck a couple every few minutes. Sam dusted everything with orange as he shoved three or four into his mouth at a time. I plucked one at a time from the plate after every five flashcards.

Clicking the space bar advanced to the next card:

"What effect do oral contraceptives have on endometrial and ovarian cancer?"

I tensed as I reached for the cheese ball I was about to earn. I had done really well not thinking about Mom today. We seemed to talk less now. No subject seemed as pressing as the obvious, but we didn't want to talk about cancer. Instead, we resorted to awkward small talk.
Why can't this deck just stick to labor and delivery stuff? Decreases the risk. That's the answer.
I crunched on my reward and swallowed hard to overcome the lump I started feeling in my throat. I felt a tear welling in the corner of my eye and pulled my sweatshirt collar up over my mouth, covering half my face and leaning closer to my computer.
If I ask how Mom is doing, she'll say "fine." If she asks how I am doing, I'll say "fine!" Everything is fine... Next card.

"What's the effect of tamoxifen on endometrial cancer?"

I should call her. It might have even been three days by now. Does she notice as much as I do? Or does she think I'm just busy with rotations and studying? I need to be better. What if she's not here this time next year, and I didn't—no, stop thinking that way... Next card.

"What are the approximate mortality rates associated with different gynecologic cancers?"

It could happen.

What if she isn't here this time next year, and I'm avoiding her because I can't be an adult about this? Because I'm sad and scared and stressed and don't want her to see it? That's why she didn't want to tell me about her cancer in the first place. She is the one, of all people, who should be allowed to be sad and scared and stressed, and for other people to see it and support her. What if she's not here this time next year, and I'm hundreds of miles away right now? Would I regret staying here? Would I regret staying in medical school? Would I regret sitting at this goddamn kitchen table right now contemplating this instead of being home?

I slammed my laptop closed and gasped for a breath. "I need to talk to you guys about something."

Dani and Sam looked up, startled and confused. Sam looked to Dani, then back to me, then back to Dani, gauging the severity of my tone. Dani closed her laptop softly, and they both waited for me to speak.

"You know how I went home?"

They both nodded.

I choked out, "Well, my mom was diagnosed with endometrial cancer a few months ago."

I went deaf, like I had my hands over my ears. I knew I was saying words—"They didn't tell me…hysterectomy…chemo…home…"—but I couldn't hear my own voice. I couldn't hear it when Dani slid out of her kitchen chair and walked over to hold me. The next thing I heard was the deep breath I finally took, then the ringing in my ears and the fan overhead and the car horn outside. And I just cried. I couldn't remember the last time I cried.

I sobbed into Dani's blue and white flannel, soaking her shoulder. When I attempted to apologize, "Your shirt…," she took its corner and wiped my makeup away.

"Stop."

"Ugh, I'm sorry, I'm gross."

"You're not."

Sam had remained quiet up until this point, with his hands folded on his lap and a contorted, but concerned, look on his face.

"I don't know how you're doing it," he chimed in.

"What?" I dabbed at my eyes with Dani's shirt, which she had removed for my use. She stood next to me in her tank top.

"I don't know how you're going through med school right now with real life stuff happening at home."

Real life stuff. Yes, I'd say cancer is pretty real. But what am I supposed to do? Just stop following my dream career path and find something else to do? If it wasn't my mom getting sick, would it have been something else? The "real life stuff"? Like Dani and her break up? Like Sam and his anxiety attacks? Doesn't everyone have "real stuff" during medical school?

"Life goes on."

It felt like a stupid thing to say. Yet, we all nodded.

"I'm calling it tonight." I folded Dani's shirt neatly before handing it back to her, as if it weren't going straight into her laundry basket.

"Let us know if you need anything." She squeezed my hand as I walked away, and Sam echoed, "Yea, let us know."

Through my bedroom door, I heard Sam's earnest and not-so-hushed whisper, "Did *you* know?"

"No, I didn't fucking know!" Dani snapped.

"Geez, I'm just asking."

I lay face up in bed and fully dressed in the dark. The ceiling fan blew air into my face which still felt damp from my tears. *I should have told them earlier. About real life stuff in general, not even just Mom. How did I fall into a habit of keeping my feelings to myself? Of closing myself off and acting like everything is fine when it isn't? They couldn't have known.*

CHAPTER 20

ABNORMAL WEIGHT GAIN

SAM

 I barreled into the kitchen, bumped into the dish rack by the sink, and sent forks and knives hurtling across the tile. The noise broke the silence so forcefully that I somewhat frightened myself and definitely scared the hell out of Anna and Dani. They had been sitting quietly in their usual seats, sipping their morning coffees. Dani was about to bring a fresh steaming cup to her lips when I made my entrance, causing her to jolt backward and spill hot liquid all over herself.

 "What the *fuck*, Sam?" She stood up to reveal a trail of caffeine down the front of her scrub top.

 "Are you okay, Sam?" Anna asked almost earnestly, ignoring Dani's plight.

 "Do we have a scale?"

 They looked at me like I was speaking a foreign language.

 "Like…to weigh yourself?" Anna clarified.

 "I thought this was going to be about evaluations again, and I was going to strangle you." Dani huffed as she pulled her soiled shirt over her head and headed to her room to change.

"Yes, to weigh myself..." I cradled my gut, pushing it out toward Anna for dramatic effect. "I've been feeling a little conch."

Dani yelled from upstairs, "*He's been feeling a little what?*"

"*Self-conscious,*" Anna yelled, "*of the weight he's put on.*"

"Oh my god, so you've noticed?" I clapped my belly with both hands. It was modest weight gain, but still significant enough for my pants to fit a little better. While I had been eating fewer true meals, frozen dinners doubled my usual caloric intake. Plus, I frequently chugged an entire protein shake between surgeries, sometimes two or three a day, which contributed to new onset gastric reflux. *Add that to the problem list.*

"We don't have a scale, but there is one in the hospital gym if you're that curious."

"Like I know where to find the hospital gym."

Anna burst out laughing.

And even if I did, I still wouldn't walk into that gym if you guaranteed me a top fifth percentile board score.

"Great, add this to the list of things I need to bring up in therapy."

I grabbed the coffee that Dani had prepared for me and bolted out the front door to work. Joking about therapy did actually make me feel better about it, even if the shrink gave me more homework for the week. My assignment: help one patient.

* * *

Sitting in the resident room on the trauma inpatient unit, I realized I had been exiled to Siberia. The unit was a frozen tundra. My ankle exposure put me at high risk for hypothermia. You could grate cheese using my standing-on-end arm hairs.

One of our trauma patients was finally being discharged, and my job was to sit in this room and "help move things along." He had to be seen by one more consulting service before he could officially leave. Social work was also coordinating his transportation to a group home, where he had been before he was shot thirteen times and admitted to the hospital.

"Helping to move things along" kind of looked like this: I sauntered from the resident room to the patient's door every twenty minutes, flexing my arms and keeping them as close to my thorax as possible to generate heat. I craned my neck to peer into the patient's room, not looking for anything in particular, and hoping he wouldn't notice.

"*Doc!*"

Shit. He caught me.

"Hello! Just checking in on you." I mustered up a jolly voice from somewhere unknown.

The poor man was shaking, draped with a thin gown and a couple of blankets that were no better than sheets.

"Doc, listen to me…I gotta favor to ask you."

"What can I do for you, sir?"

"This place where I'm going…I don't exactly have many freedoms."

I didn't know the exact details of his group home, but guessed they weren't allowed to leave.

He continued, "In the gift shop here, there are crewneck sweatshirts. When my cousin was in here last year, I saw them. Right inside the door on the left-hand side. Or at least there used to be…"

Where is this going?

"They cut off my clothes when I got here, and I don't have much. I'm not mad about it, because they saved me, but they're sending me back to the home with some scrubs that are thinner than thin. And I didn't think about it until this morning, sitting here freezing my ass off, but the group home might even be colder than here…"

While I understood the practice of cutting off people's clothes in the trauma bay, it frequently left patients without anything to wear home. We had a donation bin where employees left clothes sometimes, but if patients didn't have family to bring them anything, they were often discharged in mismatched, ill-fitting outfits or even hospital gowns.

"Doc, this is all I've got on me." He held out a twenty-dollar bill. "You know I can't get downstairs. The sweatshirts were ten dollars. I am begging you…can you get a man a crewneck? Size large? I don't even care what color. I'll never sleep again if I have to live being this cold."

This seems like a very bad idea. If this man didn't have a very broken leg, he probably could go down himself with a chaperone. If he had family close by, someone could bring him one. Social work would barely call me back about his expected transportation time, and what would they do to help with this, anyway? They'd say to check the trauma donation bin, which everyone knows is usually empty.

Fuck. I took my patient's money. "I'll be right back." *Damn it, damn it,* damn it, Sam. I damned myself with each step as I marched down to the gift shop. *They might not even have…*

As I turned into the store, there they were—a rack of plain crewneck sweatshirts. Ten dollars apiece, black or dark gray. I plucked one large black one from the middle of the rack, and I looked over my shoulder. I felt like I was shoplifting. I watched carefully as the cashier counted out my change.

"Do you need a receipt?"

"Dear Lord, *yes*, I need a receipt."

The teenager raised his eyebrows at me as his fingers waited to catch the receipt printing from the register. He barely tore it off before I snatched it out of his hand and started back toward the fourth floor. I tucked the white plastic bag containing the noncontraband under my arm.

As I handed my patient the sweatshirt and his change, showing him the receipt that accounted for every coin, I realized he was crying. He took the change and receipt in one hand and gripped my hand with the other, pulling me close to him in a half hug.

"Thank you...thank you, man."

I let him hug me, stunned. All I did was buy a cold man a sweatshirt. With his own money.

I tousled my hair as I exited his room.

The nurse manager, wrapped in a cable-knit zip-up sweater and a blanket at the workstation, snapped at me. "Hey, *you!* Yeah you."

I pointed at myself as if she'd picked me out of a massive crowd. I was the only person in the entire hallway.

"Did you do what I think you just did?"

I started to sweat a little bit.

"Excuse me?" I played dumb.

"Are you a medical student?" She accused me.

"Yes..."

"And who do you think you are taking money from a patient?"

"Whoaaa, whoa, whoa. I—"

"That is *wildly* inappropriate. I should report you. You know that's a huge liability? You should be written up."

Is this lady serious right now? For the sweatshirt? Did she see the man crying?

"Listen—"

"No, honey, you listen—we don't take money from patients. Who is your supervisor?"

My blood was boiling. It was the first time I felt warm all day.

"Ma'am," I stated firmly, "are you cold right now?"

"Is this some kind of joke? Yes, I'm freezing!"

"*Well,*" I started, "I'm quite cold, too. Now imagine you're a patient who has been through multiple surgeries. You're anemic. You have a thin hospital gown and thin sheet and thin blanket to cover you and nothing else. You're about to be discharged to a facility where you have *no* freedoms, and it's a place that's supposed to help you get *better,* but you can't even *sleep* because it is *freezing cold, every night.*"

I was careful to not raise my voice *too* much, but, internally, I was screaming. I continued, "Could you *imagine* if someone on your *care* team had the *decency* to show you some *humanity* to run *downstairs* to grab you a *ten-dollar gift store sweatshirt.*"

She sat there and continued scowling at me but said nothing.

I leveled my tone. "My supervisor's name is Dr. Kelly. Pager number is 5708. Please let her know that I took the patient's money to buy him a sweatshirt—at his request. 5708."

As I turned into the resident room, I realized Intern Alex must have come upstairs while I was in the gift shop. She'd heard the whole exchange. She was smirking and started to slow clap.

"Look at you, Sam."

* * *

Adrenaline pumped through my veins for the rest of the day. My walk home turned into a jog. My legs simply decided they wanted to move faster. I couldn't even help myself. When I got to the house, I dropped my bag inside the door, changed my clothes, and went right back outside for a run. Yes, a run. Approximately one mile. Maybe slightly less. There were hills, but I triumphed over them. *I helped a patient today, and now I'm going to help myself.* I sucked wind like a top model Dyson vacuum, but I made it back to the front stoop. *Who needs a hospital gym?*

The energy didn't stop there—I pushed on. After a quick shower, I cleaned my room, did my laundry, and picked up my things scattered around the house. I crushed the last block of study questions for the Shelf exam with a few days to spare. By the time the girls got home, I was settled comfortably into my seat at the kitchen table, cleaning out my email inbox that I hadn't touched since 'Nam.

Dani sat down across from me to use her laptop while Anna shuffled around, tidying. Anna cracked open the dishwasher to inspect whether it had been run. She slid out the top rack, stuck her face close to the glassware to verify cleanliness, and begin emptying it. After pulling out two glasses from the front, she paused. "Something's not right."

I smirked and continued to scroll through my emails.

"What?" Dani asked, perplexed.

Sticking her head deeper into the dishwasher, Anna questioned, "Where's the mug?"

"What?" Dani repeated.

"Sam, where's your mug?"

Still smirking, I stated, "In the cabinet."

They both stared at me in confusion.

I followed up matter-of-factly, "I washed it."

Dani's jaw dropped to the floor, and she reached over for a high five. Anna started to slow clap. We all exchanged silly hoots and hollers, celebrating this minor victory. *I am crushing today.* When the laughing died down, Anna returned to the dishwasher.

"Sam…"

"Yes?"

"Why didn't you empty the rest of the dishwasher?

"Baby steps, sweet girl. Baby steps."

CHAPTER 21

HEART FAILURE

DANI

"You better start giving out yours."

Mr. Fruit Cup's words rang in my head while I sifted through a stack of unused thank you notes and greeting cards. None of the stationary in the depths of my desk drawers seemed appropriate. I wanted a card that was somewhat professional, but not too corporate-looking. One that was generic, but not too plain.

If I am going to write a note to a patient, what should it look like? Ugh, screw it.

I scrapped the idea altogether and tried to focus on studying. The next day was my last day of the rotation, the day after that was a dedicated study day for Shelf, and the day after that was doomsday. Having scored a little less than average on the practice test, I wasn't feeling particularly confident going into the real exam. I knew I needed to maximize my study time over the next two days. "Mr. Fruit Cup," I scribbled at the top of my clean notebook page where I was supposed to be transcribing definitions, criteria, and management plans that would be etched into my mind.

I shook my head and stretched my arms above my head, attempting to bring myself back to awareness of the task at hand. I restarted the video on hyponatremia, but only made it fourteen minutes in before realizing I never even started paying attention. Studying felt impossible—hopeless, even.

How can I give out pieces of myself when I feel like a shell?

After deciding to take a lap outside to clear my head, I found myself in the greeting card aisle of the grocery store down the street. Greeting cards, to me, always felt like a silly and antiquated form of communication. Was the sentiment *that* sentimental if it was written by a stranger and you paid $4.99 for it? I guess if the stranger was able to capture your feelings in words better than you could, it was worth the price of a coffee—especially if you weren't used to talking about your emotions.

I couldn't remember the last time that I really let myself feel, or the last time I bought a greeting card, for that matter. The offered categories didn't fit my situation at all.

Should I browse the "Good Luck" section? Sympathy? Humor? Friendship? If there isn't a section called "For Patient, From Medical Student," maybe I should rethink this?

I floundered on whether writing a note to a patient was appropriate at all as I picked up one card after another, glancing at the insides and grimacing, rolling my eyes, or shaking my head. Nothing seemed right. Obviously, I knew there were lines not meant to be crossed, but it was going to be our last day together. I felt like there needed to be some sort of conclusion, some way to acknowledge that my time with Mr. Fruit Cup was important.

The cashier rang up a card that said "blank inside" on the plastic sleeve. That was the only option that accurately reflected how I felt in that moment.

* * *

The weight of the card in my pocket encumbered me the entire morning. It felt illicit, like I had a secret message to deliver or was carrying classified information. Knowing I would see Mr. Fruit Cup many times over the course of the day, I didn't want to rush and give it to him first thing in the morning. What if he mentioned it to the team on rounds? That would have been mortifying. Or what if someone saw it and asked him what it was? Would he show them?

Mr. Fruit Cup was finally at the top of a waitlist for a rehab facility. We weren't doing very much to manage his care at that time; he would be leaving soon. Although he was still weak, he would tell anyone that asked that he was feeling better than he had for months.

When I walked into his room at the end of the day, we both knew it was the last time. Longitudinal care was not built into the medical school curriculum. Tomorrow, I would no longer be taking care of Mr. Fruit Cup. I wouldn't even be in this hospital anymore, moving on to an affiliated location. I would have new patients, and, likely, would never see Mr. Fruit Cup again.

"This is it, huh?" he asked.

I nodded quietly, sat on the edge of his bed, and handed him the note.

His hands looked skeletal, his skin stretched like plastic wrap over his knuckles as he fumbled with the crisp envelope and extracted the card. His fingertips stroked the abstract design printed on the front: swirls of cobalt blue and metallic steel in a sea of pearly white and gray, like marble. He smiled at it with appreciation. When he opened the card, his eyes darted up and down my handwritten message. I had taken care to scrawl neatly, knowing my typical chicken-scratch was illegible, but he didn't seem to be able to read it.

I reached for the card, "Mr. Fruit Cup, why don't you let me…"

He sighed, "Sorry, Doctah Dani. I don't read real good."

I felt a pang in my chest. After all we had been through, that had never occurred to me.

I smiled with reassurance. "Don't worry, I was hoping I could read it out loud anyway."

I straightened my back and cleared my throat dramatically, pounding on my chest with a closed fist as if I were about to deliver an official speech or theatrical monologue. He sat up a little in his bed, adjusting his pillow around his lower back, and I began cheerfully: "Mr. Fruit Cup. In our short time together, you have taught me so much about communication, respect, and tr-trust."

When I stammered, I felt him tense up immediately. I told myself I wouldn't get emotional, but speaking the words was proving way more challenging than writing them. I knew that his eyes were locked firmly on my face; I could feel those, too.

I spoke more softly. "We, um…we have shared moments of sadness and, ha, frustration," I looked up, and he cracked a smile, "but also, many of light-hearted laughter and deep personal reflection." Hot tears began blurring my vision. I wouldn't look up again; I couldn't.

My voice was cracking now. "You have touched my heart," I whimpered, "I will never forget being a part of your care team." I sniffled and breathed out heavily. *Keep going, Dani.*

I managed to muster an ounce of composure and finished steadily. "I hope that wherever you may go, you continue to share your smile and your soul with the people around you. Love, Student Doctor Dani." I closed the card and met his gaze. He was clutching his hospital gown over his heart and weeping silently.

I offered him my upturned palm. He didn't even look at it, but instead leaned forward and slowly, shakily, carefully, tenderly wrapped his arms around me and buried his head into my shoulder. Jay's words from my very first day of the rotation came back to me: *"Don't get too close."* Instead, I held on to the man I once feared, while he held on to the white coat he once feared, too.

CHAPTER 22

SHORTNESS OF BREATH

―

ANNA

My final week on Ob-Gyn had been hitting me hard, and my last day was no exception. Running the resident clinic, the two interns and I had just crushed a hectic morning, one that would make you raise an eyebrow at the scheduling process. *Another double booking? Who runs this place?*

I had learned to manage bread-and-butter patients with ease. Dani joked that I was a "pap queen," having performed far more smears than the average student-doctor-serf. It felt like a handsome reward when the interns sent me to the OR to help with an afternoon case instead of staying in clinic.

"It's your last day! Go get some more OR time and get out of here early."

The surgery was an add-on to the schedule, and I had no time to read about it. They said that I should just run up to the third floor and find the staffing resident for a quick briefing. I half-jogged to pre-op. Scanning the board, I found the only Ob-Gyn case listed—a D&E. Dilation and evacuation. A surgical abortion. I felt a familiar drop in my stomach. *Even hysterectomy number twenty would have been better than this.*

I had already endured a few shifts in the family planning clinic and had become accustomed to the difficult conversations, the jarring noise of the vacuum, and the anticlimactic medical option (take this pill now, then tomorrow these two…). It was graphic and provocative and unsettling—I didn't *like* it—but it was a "valuable learning experience."

I walked in circles around the bays, searching for the staffing resident, when a nurse took pity on me and asked if I needed help. She wasn't sure who was staffing the case, but the patient was in bay six.

The patient… I should probably introduce myself to the patient. I don't need another awkward first meeting between-the-legs, but I guess this would be happening in the OR…

Patient-in-six had magnificent dark hair, uniformly brilliant and neatly styled. Her fingernails appeared freshly painted and glossed, pale pink. She looked fit, her toned arms poking out from her oversized hospital gown that still failed to hide her modestly pregnant belly. She was visibly anxious, the color completely gone from her face.

Geez. How uncomfortable it must be—for any nervous pre-op patient—to hear: "Hi, I'm the medical student working with your team…" They usually don't even know their team has medical students. We just add stress to already stressful situations. Just so we can learn.

Patient-in-six simply nodded silently through my rehearsed primer.

I'm not even sure she caught a word I said…

I dejectedly located the physician's work room near the ORs. I found it occupied by a single scrub cap, which, of course, was fitted on Bitchy-Rachel.

Just my luck. She's the resident on the case. What do I say? I'm here to scrub with you? Why does that sound so dumb all of a sudden? Scrub? Scrub in?

She was furiously typing, and I hesitated to interrupt. I didn't say anything, but she whipped around and sternly commanded: "Sit down."

I obeyed like an anxious puppy with only so many tricks mastered, anticipating a scolding from the tone of her voice. Bitchy-Rachel wheeled her chair so close to mine that the knees of our scrubs were almost touching. It was the first time I noticed the blue of her irises; the color was weary, the pigment appearing almost diluted—glacial, icy.

She gripped me with her eyes. "You don't have to do anything if you're not comfortable, and you can leave at any time, just to be clear, okay?"

I nodded, still not quite understanding why she spoke with such gravity.

"This case is...tough." She paused.

"Okay..." I filled in the silence.

"This, um, abortion...it's...*just* within the law. And because of that, it's, uh, outside most providers' comfort zones." She fidgeted, clearly uncomfortable herself. I knew Bitchy-Rachel didn't have much choice in the matter. The attending accepted the cases; Bitchy-Rachel simply performed them under supervision.

She continued, choosing her words carefully, "The procedure *had* to be scheduled for today, otherwise the baby would have to be carried to term."

As a medical student, this was one of the rare times I could have taken a free pass and gone back to clinic. But I didn't.

I gulped. "I understand."

It could be a valuable learning experience?

The OR was frigid, as always. Bitchy-Rachel positioned herself on a stool between the patient's thighs, spread and elevated. I stood slightly behind her and to the side, delicately tucked within the V-shaped surgical field and hyperaware of the patient's foot, draped and resting in a stirrup only inches from my ear. I mentally prepared to hand the chief surgical instruments. But then she picked up the speculum and forceps from the tray herself.

Bitchy-Rachel's arms were noticeably trembling. After a moment of desperate grasping, she pulled out a tiny leg. It was pale and slippery and did not require a magnifying glass to count its five toes. I held out the collection basin.

She went back in. The steel of the forceps racked the steel of the speculum. Minutes flashed past on the wall timer; Bitchy-Rachel was struggling to find a grip. Beads of sweat formed at her temple under her face shield. The clinking sounds ran closer and closer together as the exasperation climbed. I generally knew better than to invade the area in which a surgeon was working, but I couldn't watch anymore.

I ever-so-slowly and ever-so-cautiously extended my hand toward hers, nudging my gloved knuckles under the cold forceps and gingerly grasping the speculum to steady it. Bitchy-Rachel froze...then sat up a bit, relaxed her shoulders, and rested her hand on mine.

It was only a moment, then, before the second leg came out, followed by the torso and head all at once. I had the basin ready to take it all away. Instruments clanked and gowns ripped as the staff tore them from their bodies, but we were otherwise quiet.

Bitchy-Rachel and I made our way back to the work room. Our bodies placed themselves in the same knee-to-knee configuration we were in before. The hum of the prehistoric computers was the only sound. I could swear specks of dust were suspended in the air, like time had stopped. The bustle of pre-op on the other side of the door ceased to exist.

"Are you okay?" Her voice was steady, but her hands were still shaking.

"I-I think so…are you…okay?" I heard my voice quiver.

"I'll be fine." She looked down at her fingers, clenching and unclenching, tightly and repetitively.

The words just came out: "That must have been really hard for you."

I mentally slapped myself. *Don't piss her off. Leave it alone and know your place…*

But she nodded silently, then acknowledged quietly: "Every day here is hard for me."

She moved her hands to her belly.

Fetal demise, emergency C-sections, surgical abortions… it had never occurred to me how distressing it must be for an Ob-Gyn resident who is also pregnant. I tried not to stare at the single tear welling in the corner of her eye.

"You should go. I have a million pages to return…" She pulled a small stack of papers from her scrub pocket and started shuffling them. "Do you have anyone to talk to on your way home?"

"Yeah…" *Good thing I'm working on the whole "opening up" thing. I'll have to tell Sam and Dani about this.*

I was eager to get home to them, but something didn't sit well with me about just leaving in that moment. *Why can't you just drop it, Anna?*

"Do…*you* have anyone to talk to?"

Bitchy-Rachel paused, staring at the tattered lists in her hand.

I held my breath when she turned around and carefully laid her papers face down on the desk behind her. She looked me dead in the eyes.

"I have avoided bringing work home since I had a miscarriage last year. We—my husband and I—we were completely devastated. I don't want to worry him with stories from the hospital, so I keep them all to myself."

She broke eye contact to glance at her feet. "All of the most difficult moments…like today…I let them fester. And all the beautiful moments…I don't let myself appreciate them." She exhaled slowly. "How could I? How could I let myself be optimistic, for even a moment, when I know everything that could possibly go wrong?"

She found my eyes again and bit her cheek. "In the process of trying to protect myself and our new baby, I've allowed myself to forget why I wanted to be a doctor in the first place. I know I haven't been the kindest to the people around me. I am working on being better. And I'm sorry."

The sincerity in her voice was foreign and striking. "Thanks for your help today, Anna."

I didn't phone anyone on my thirty-five-minute commute home. I encountered the usual cacophony of rush hour—horns wailing on Main Street, commuter buses whirring past, music booming from a sports car that had no place in the city—but all I could hear was the quiet of OR-3.

Later that night, I felt ready to verbalize what had happened to Sam and Dani. I realized, as I told the story at the kitchen table, that I called the main character "Rachel."

CHAPTER 23

SHOCK

DANI

Well, we survived Shelf round one. What a weekend.

Rubbing my eyes, I powered up my laptop at the kitchen table. Anna and Sam were already there, computers open and focused on their tasks. Although I'd slept like a rock, I would need a few nights to recover from the shock of Friday's exam and the weekend of heavy partying that followed. That type of socializing could only happen between rotations, so I had to take advantage. I didn't bounce back as quickly as they did. Old age, Sam would say.

Sunday offered the opportunity to recoup and prepare for my new rotation that would start promptly the next morning. It felt like weeks had passed since my tearful goodbye with Mr. Fruit Cup, but it had only been three days. Part of me wanted to roll into the hospital for rounds, to continue my morning routine. It felt almost unfair to be moved to another rotation when I had built relationships with my patients and started becoming comfortable.

I felt compelled to check Mr. Fruit Cup's progress notes since I left.

Did he finally get discharged to subacute rehab?
I typed in his patient ID from my pocket planner into the search tab, then clicked enter. I looked down to sip my coffee as the banner appeared on the screen.

DECEASED PATIENT; Code: Not Ordered

I choked and nearly spit all over my computer as I looked up. My eyes darted back and forth over the message.
Am I looking at the right patient?
I frantically verified the details I had memorized long ago.
That's definitely his full name and birth date…
I clicked refresh again, gripping the end of the table and biting my lip. The same gray banner reappeared.

DECEASED PATIENT; Code: Not Ordered

A burning pit formed in my stomach, and heat rose into my chest.
He was stable… He was better. How did this happen?
Not realizing that I had been holding my breath, I gasped for air as I opened his last note.

Death Summary: Patient experienced septic shock secondary to bacteremia.

No. How could this happen? Septic shock? How did he get an infection?
I frantically scrolled through the pages of notes and data from the few days prior.
He developed a fever the day after I left the service? Like, the very next day? Who rounded on him that morning?

I went back to the beginning, to the first day I wasn't there to see Mr. Fruit Cup. Jay had rounded on him that morning. His note was succinct, noting a new fever of unknown source. He ordered a number of tests to determine where the infection originated. I quickly reviewed all of the results. *He got a hospital acquired infection.*

I felt like we gave it to him, like I had personally infected him. The system had failed him. *If he'd had a bed at the rehab facility sooner, would this have been prevented? If he had cooperated with PT a day earlier...if someone had listened to him or been more patient.* I clicked to the next note.

Event Note: Patient stepped up to ICU for worsening respiratory status in the setting of metabolic acidosis.

Shit. If he got moved up to the ICU, he would have had a whole new team. New nurses, a new attending, new residents, maybe even a new medical student. I'm sure he didn't like that. He was just getting comfortable, and it took so long for us to get to that point.

Event Note: Patient is agitated, refusing food and meds. Wants to be left alone. Discussed behavior with IMC attending physician who said this is not unusual for this patient.

Not unusual? At this point, it was unusual. He had been taking his meds for weeks by then. He would have taken them if I had been there. He trusted me. What if I had been there?

Event Note: Uncooperative with all care measures. Given Haldol 5 mg IM at 15:30.

Those assholes! They drugged him to calm him down? Did anyone ask him why he was agitated? Did anyone even try to talk to him?

The next few pages in his chart detailed his rapidly worsening condition. One note stood out among the critical care labels.

Palliative Care Note:

Palliative care was consulted for this seventy-year-old gentleman with multi-drug resistant bacteremia of unknown source and multiple comorbid conditions, refusing further treatment.

Patient was determined to have the capacity to make medical decisions. When asked why he was refusing therapy, patient expressed frustration with communication between himself and his medical team. Patient asked to return to IMC unit and did not understand why he was moved; asked if he was being punished for his behavior.

After a lengthy discussion and positive reassurance, the patient is amenable to beginning antibiotic therapy. Of note, the patient divulged that he lost his wife a few years ago and has a long history of PTSD. Patient is not interested in counseling at this time but agreed to speak with the hospital chaplain.

Discussed further goals of care with patient. Patient expressed understanding of his diagnosis and prognosis. Patient **does not** want any heroic or extraordinary measures to keep him alive. **Do not resuscitate, do not intubate.** Will discuss pain management recommendations with the primary team.

I spent a total of ninety minutes on this consultation. Sixty minutes of this time was spent in counseling.

I felt the tension in my shoulders loosening.
Someone listened to him. He told them about Margot. He gave them a piece, maybe his last one.
I breezed through the last few notes which chronicled his decline, despite him accepting treatment. I returned to the death summary, the final note in his chart. I read through the physical exam, sick to my stomach, picturing Mr. Fruit Cup, my friend.

Physical Exam at Time of Death:

General: Male patient lying in bed.

Eyes: Fixed, dilated pupils. Absent corneal reflex.

Respiratory: No chest rise. Absent breath sounds.

Cardiovascular: Absent heart sounds. Absent carotid pulse.

Neuro: No response to painful stimuli.

How many times did I sit at his bedside? See the life in his electric green eyes? Listen to his heart? Feel his pulse?
I read it again.

Neuro: No response to painful stimuli.

My own nausea and aching and agony quietly dissipated. *He didn't feel any pain.*

I heard his voice clearly in my memory: *"Someday, I'll be back with Margot, and I won't feel any pain at all."*

I closed my laptop, then my planner, with the "Dr. Dani" sticky note still clinging to the cover. I ran my fingers over the shaky handwriting.

Out of the corner of my eye, I saw that Anna noticed my unusual behavior. She watched quietly until a tear rolled down my face.

"You okay?"

I inhaled slowly.

"He died."

Sam looked up from his computer. Anna touched my hand from across the table.

"Dani," she inhaled deeply, then sighed, "having this patient on your first rotation was probably the best thing that could have happened to you."

Because he died? Because now I know what that feels like? Now it won't hurt as much the next time?

I sniffled. "Why?"

"I guess...well..." She shrugged and shook her head. "He reminded you of why we're doing this. I feel like we forget that medicine is about so much more than just the *medicine*. It's not about memorizing drug doses and trending labs and writing progress notes."

Sam nodded solemnly, looking deep in thought.

"Medicine is about *all* the parts of the human experience." Anna swallowed hard and continued, "And a simple interaction can ripple through not only a patient's life, but our lives, too."

Anna's mom...Bitchy-Rachel...the woman with the D&E... the cold trauma patient...

Sam finally spoke.

"Sometimes all it takes is a fruit cup."

EPILOGUE

DANI

"Dr. Foster?"

One week into my intern year, I was still wildly uncomfortable with my new title. My long white coat said it—"Danielle Foster, MD"—but it felt like a stretch. Last week, I was a medical student. This week, I held multiple pagers, prescribed medications, made clinical decisions, and even called time-of-death.

Sure, it was exciting, but I also constantly worried that I would make a mistake. Maybe that would get easier. Tonight, though, I was more focused on getting home. I had a date. Having just signed out my patients to the night team, I was high tailing it out the door when the charge nurse caught me. I spun around on my heels.

"Hey, what's up?"

"Sorry, I know you're on your way out..."

"That's okay, what's going on?"

Please be quick...

"I just wanted to say that I know this week on the unit has been a bit, uh, devastating," he paused, "but you're doing great. The ICU is a tough place to start."

My expression softened.

"Thank you for saying that."

"Have a good weekend, doc."

Doc. So weird.

Traffic was kinder than it had been, and I pulled up to my new home with some daylight still lingering. Playing catch up with all my adult friends, I had purchased a tiny house just outside the city. The front door opened easily; I missed the finicky latch at the old house. I hastily threw leftovers in the microwave and sat down at my table: a large, reclaimed farmhouse piece that perfectly filled the dining room. Though only one seat was occupied, the setup left plenty of room to grow. Propping my phone up on an unpacked box, I dialed in.

Sam and Anna's faces popped up in an instant.

"Hiiiiii team!" Sam sang. He sat at his own new kitchen table—a narrow countertop in his shoebox apartment in some urban high-rise building. His knees just about touched his oven from where he sat. His hair was freshly chopped, and his button-down shirt that he wore to clinic fit him better than any clothes I had ever seen him in.

"How was everyone's day?" Anna chirped. Her table of choice was a modern glass top on brushed gold legs. The apartment behind her looked spotless and refined—fully lived-in, though she had only just settled.

"Oh, it was glorious!"

"Living the dream."

"Excellent, excellent."

We had only been apart for a short time, but I missed our routine. The end of medical school disrupted a lot of our normalcy. We matched into residency in March, graduated in May, and went our separate ways in June.

Anna moved closer to home; her mom was in remission, and Anna wanted to spend as much time as she could with her family during residency. Sam, somewhat inadvertently, ended up where his both of his moms had trained. They'd been shockingly supportive of his decision to become a pediatrician (but were still pushing for a critical care fellowship).

"I caught three babies today!" Anna announced.

"Woof," Sam retorted, "you know the fresh ones usually aren't my favorite, but I had some cute newborns in clinic today."

I wish I had felt the divine inspiration Sam had after his pediatrics rotation or had a deep personal connection like Anna had with Ob-Gyn after everything with her mom. I landed on internal medicine—the rotation I'd initially dreaded the most—without one hundred percent certainty that it was what I wanted. But I'd come to realize that so much of medicine was about operating with uncertainty. And by being a generalist, I would encounter patients with so many different stories. Who knows, maybe I'd end up doing a palliative care fellowship someday.

I chimed in, "Well, my first patient this week had a seizure as soon as he got to the floor. Before I could even meet him."

"Good start, Dan," Sam quipped.

"Yup," I chuckled, "but he ended up being fine! I ordered Ativan like a big girl doctor, and the seizure broke!"

"Wow, okay, but actually, I would have shit myself."

Anna snickered. "Remember when you almost shit your pants in the OR?"

Sam choked on the coffee he was sipping, spewing liquid from his nose onto himself. Almost two years later, he was finally able to laugh about it.

Anna snorted as she wiped tears from her eyes. "Or Dani, how about when your underwear ripped?"

"Stop," Sam begged as he tried catching his breath, "I'm aspirating."

We cackled at the memories; our previous embarrassments and fears seemed a little less consequential now. We didn't reminisce for long. Anna had to prepare a Grand Rounds talk. Sam was on call the next day, and I had to work, too.

"You know, we could all still quit and do something else…"

"Shut up, Sam."

We had made it so far, but there wasn't exactly an "end" in sight: years of residency, board exams, maybe fellowship applications. We were no longer called "students," but that's what we would be for the rest of our lives.

We signed off, and I pulled my notebook from my bag. Flipping to the very back, I made a mental note to order a new one. The pages were filled with stories from the past two years. After Mr. Fruit Cup died, I'd started writing every day, even if it was just a few sentences. Putting words on paper helped me process my medical school experiences. I found that the more I wrote, the more I felt, and the more likely I was to give away my pieces. I started feeling whole again.

Dragging my pen across the page, I wrote *"devastating"* across the top and underlined it.

Underneath, I jotted in a column:

traumatic
distressing
overwhelming

I paused, clicking my pen, then added off to the side:

captivating
striking
beautiful

In the last bit of space in the notebook, I scribbled:

Practicing medicine is devastating in every meaning of the word. Sometimes it's challenging to acknowledge both sides—the bad and the beautiful. But maybe that's how you learn to thrive.

ACKNOWLEDGEMENTS

To my best friends who inspired my main characters—thank you for getting me through med school. You are already incredible doctors, and I love you.

To my family and friends—thank you for the pep talks, welcome distractions, and confidence in me when I struggled to find it myself.

To my mentors before, during, and after med school—thank you for being coaches for life.

To the New Degree Press team: Eric, Diedre, Carol—thank you for being patient with a medical student trying to learn how to doctor and write a book at the same time.

To all my supporters—thanks for making it happen.

Rhonda Allen
The Ambler Family—Amanda, Jon, & Levi
Richard & Zaiga Antonetti
Mary Bacon
The Barbieri Family
Sarah Berg
The Bonderenko Family
Elizabeth Borowiec
Notorious Bose, MD

Gina Campbell
Kimberly Canny
The Carew Family—Todd, Melanie, Olivia, Lilly, & Brooke
Kelly Carr
Patsy Casalino
Christopher Christiano
Micki Cirillo
Jared & Kayla Cohen
Jacob Colver
Juliette Conte
The Cooney Family—Dan, Lori, Nathan, & Matthew
Dan Corry
Danica Cutshall
Olivia Damico
The Denofrio Family—Allison, Michael, Toria, & Tebony
Michael DeSanto
Mike DiFrancesco
Erin Drakeley
The Dzinski Family—Bernie, MaryAnn, Andrew, & Julia
Kristen Edwards
The Fappiano Family—Cary, Mark, Marny, & Corey
The Fappiano Family—Gene, Michelle, & Sami
Lauren Gagliardi
Lani Galloway
Sherrie Gemmell
Ed Generali
Benjamin Greenspun
The Hamel Family—Carla, Rick, Rachel, & Jeremy
Gina Harrison
Brian Hayes & Tara Burke
Wayne Hogrefe
Lynda Houghtaling

Kyle Humphrey
Julia Jester
Hannah Kelly
Carol Knight
Pei-Ying Kobres
Eric Koester
Micaela LaRose
Angela Lauretano
Kevin Leger
Jacob Loesche
Bob & Francine LoRusso
Geert Martens & Ray Murray
Jodie McGarrity
The McGrenery Family—Tom, Sue, Ryan, & Maegan
Dan Merenstein
Caitlin Merley
Maggie Moran
Julie Moseley
Kathy & Keith Mosgrove
Bridget Mullen
J. V. Nable
Tina Nave
Patricia Neville
Crystal Park
Rani Patel
Kyle Pelkey
Dan & Mary Pelkey
Olivia Pelletier
Idanis Perez-Alvarez
Joe Polletta
Katie Priestley
Mike & Meg Ramirez

Carmine Razza & Paula Keegan
Marc & Christine Razza
Louie & Kathy Razza
The Razza Family—Craig, Marta, Kristina, & Adam
The Rinaldi Family—Pat, Cathie, Elizabeth, & Adriana
The Santopietro Family—Joe, Julie, Sabrina, & Paige
Nevada Schadler
Christina Sharkey & Thomas Brooke
Stacy Shimp
Steven Siemieniak
Dana Sievers
Dan Silkman
Mary Simms
Nicole Sipfle
The Smith-Breiner Family—Kirsten, Erin, Cavan, & Paloma
Cris Spinner
Amanda Steinfeld
Kate Stolzer
Gary & Tracy Sullivan
Lloyd Tannenbaum
Alexander Theos
Cate Tompkins
Gina Tremaglio
Tate Vernon
Alex Viso & Ryan Freeman
Jacqueline Voegeli
Morgan Watts
Nicholas Wegener
Paige Wilde

APPENDIX

AUTHOR'S NOTE

Boyle, P. "Medical School Applicants and Enrollments Hit Record Highs; Underrepresented Minorities Lead the Surge." AAMC, December 8, 2021. https://www.aamc.org/news-insights/medical-school-applicants-and-enrollments-hit-record-highs-underrepresented-minorities-lead-surge.

Brazeau, C. M., T. Shanafelt, S. J. Durning, F. S. Massie, A. Eacker, C. Moutier, ... L. N. Dyrbye. "Distress Among Matriculating Medical Students Relative to the General Population." *Academic Medicine* 89, no. 11 (2014): 1520–1525.

www.ingramcontent.com/pod-product-compliance
Lightning Source LLC
LaVergne TN
LVHW012016060526
838201LV00061B/4332